D1348350

THOUGHT AND REALITY

Lines of Thought

Short philosophical books

General editors: Peter Ludlow and Scott Sturgeon

Published in association with the Aristotelian Society

THOUGHT AND REALITY

MICHAEL DUMMETT

CLARENDON PRESS · OXFORD

OXFORD

UNIVERSITY PRESS

Great Clarendon Street, Oxford OX2 6DP

Oxford University Press is a department of the University of Oxford.
It furthers the University's objective of excellence in research, scholarship,
and education by publishing worldwide in

Oxford New York

Auckland Cape Town Dar es Salaam Hong Kong Karachi
Kuala Lumpur Madrid Melbourne Mexico City Nairobi
New Delhi Shanghai Taipei Toronto

With offices in

Argentina Austria Brazil Chile Czech Republic France Greece
Guatemala Hungary Italy Japan Poland Portugal Singapore
South Korea Switzerland Thailand Turkey Ukraine Vietnam

Oxford is a registered trademark of Oxford University Press
in the UK and in certain other countries

Published in the United States
by Oxford University Press Inc., New York

British Library Cataloguing in Publication Data

Data available

Library of Congress Cataloging in Publication Data
Dummett, Michael A. E.
Thought and reality / Michael Dummett.
p. cm. —(Lines of thought : short philosophical books)
Includes index.
ISBN-13: 978–0–19–920727–5 (alk. paper)
ISBN-10: 0–19–920727–5 (alk. paper)
1. Truth. I. Title.
BD171.D86 2006
121—dc22 2006027700

Typeset by Laserwords Private Limited, Chennai, India
Printed in Great Britain
on acid-free paper by
Biddles Ltd., King's Lynn, Norfolk

ISBN 0–19–920727–5   978–0–19–920727–5

1 3 5 7 9 10 8 6 4 2

Preface

When, in 1996, I was invited to give some Gifford Lectures at the University of St Andrews, I asked whether it was a requirement that I publish them. 'It is not a requirement,' was the answer, 'but it is usual to do so.' Well, I thought, that will be a task for the later part of my retirement. I had in advance envisaged retirement as a period in which I should be my own master: free to work at what I chose, at whatever pace I chose. I found it quite unlike that. I have been retired for thirteen years now, and this is the first time I have felt myself free to do whatever work I like. As is shown by the craters on the Moon and on all other planetary satellites that have been inspected by space probes, those bodies have been bombarded by meteoroids and rocks flying around in space. In my experience, a retired academic is like a planetary satellite: he is bombarded by requests: 'Would you contribute to a volume I am editing on . . . ?', 'I hope you will come and give us a lecture on one of the following dates . . .', 'We shall be very interested if you would deliver a paper at the conference I am organizing on . . .'. Each thinks, 'Now he is retired, he will have plenty of time'. Oxford University has indeed left me severely alone, asking nothing of me since I laid down my academic duties; no one else has. There has not been a moment in those thirteen years when I have not been writing something under pressure. I admit that some of the pressure was self-imposed, such as composing my *Principles of Electoral Reform* and the English version of my *Origins of Analytical Philosophy*. The most laborious of these has been the compilation, with my co-author John McLeod, of our *History of Games Played with the Tarot Pack*. My heartfelt thanks go to John McLeod and the publisher, Mellen Press, and to John McLeod for making this possible. Originally, I proposed to write the whole book by myself; had I done so, I should not have finished yet. It was an inspired idea to ask John McLeod to help me, a great expert whom otherwise I should have had to consult a good deal.

Because so much got in the way, I have been unable until now to turn to revising the Gifford Lectures that I gave in 1996–7. I have revised them only lightly; I have in the main avoided importing into them views I now hold but did not hold when giving the lectures. There are exceptions in Chapters 1 and 2. I have now treated as independent the question whether the proposition expressed by uttering a declarative sentence depends on the time of utterance and the question whether or not temporal indicators should be treated as sentential operators. When I gave the Gifford Lectures, I thought, as Prior thought, that the two questions hung together; but it now seems to me clear that, even if we treat the adverb 'tomorrow' as an operator 'it will be the case tomorrow that', we remain free to treat utterances on different days of a sentence in which it occurs as expressing different propositions. Furthermore, when I delivered the lectures, I believed it to be a substantive question whether or not the proposition expressed by uttering a sentence depends on the time of utterance. I now consider it to be a matter of convenience, heavily weighted in favour of an affirmative answer. I now think that the concept of a proposition has a less integral role in a theory of meaning than I did when I gave the lectures, and have adapted Chapters 1 and 2 accordingly. There is also a change in Chapter 8, signalled there. When I gave the lectures, I thought that I had given an adequate reason for believing in the existence of God, as a mind comprehending the whole of reality, and thereby constituting it in being. But I thought quite different considerations needed to be invoked in order to argue that God has a will, either for us (a will that we should act in such-and-such ways) or for Himself. I no longer think that this needs appeal to quite different considerations, and in the present text have explained why not.

There is a second reason for my delay in publishing the lectures. For long I felt uneasy about the treatment of time in those lectures; they represented a transitional phase in my thinking about the subject. Chapters 5–7 express views I no longer hold. It will naturally be asked why I am publishing them as I gave them, if I no longer agree with them. I indeed long hesitated to do so; I thought I ought to revise them to accord with what I was subsequently coming to think, but held back because I did not feel sure *what* I thought. Since I published my Dewey Lectures as *Truth and the Past*, my worry about my treatment of time in the Gifford Lectures has lifted. I felt I need not demur from publishing the Gifford Lectures more or less as they stood, since in the Dewey Lectures I had set out a modification of the views[1] I had expressed in the earlier set. All the same, if I was sure that I had improved on my earlier thoughts, why put those earlier thoughts into print? The answer is that I am *not* sure. All turns on what notion of truth is appropriate to a justificationist theory of meaning. The question has worried me for many years. For a time I had believed that the justificationist must be an anti-realist about the past, a conclusion about which I always felt uneasy. The Gifford Lectures firmly repudiate this; but the conception of truth that they propose does not make so conciliatory an advance in a realist direction as does that proposed in the Dewey Lectures. So the two sets of lectures offer a choice between two possible conceptions of truth, conceptions that I hope I have succeeded in delineating with reasonable clarity. Because I do not really know what is the right conception, I have thought it possibly not unhelpful to publish my Gifford Lectures essentially as they were delivered.

There are two differences between the two conceptions of truth. In the Gifford Lectures, a proposition is reckoned to be true just in case *we*, as we are or were, are or were in a position to establish it to hold good; my present standpoint, as stated in the Dewey

---

[1] There is further modification in my reply to Christopher Peacocke in *Mind* ('The Justificationist's Response to a Realist', *Mind*, 114 July 2005, 671–88).

Lectures, is that it is true just in case *anyone suitably placed in time and space* would be or have been in such a position. The difference has an evidently far-reaching effect: far more propositions will be rendered true under the Dewey than under the Gifford conception. For instance, the colour of a flower must be determinate, since such an observer would necessarily have evidence for it, even if such evidence is not available to us. The second difference is that, in the Gifford Lectures, the past and the future are not treated symmetrically, whereas, under my present interpretation, they are. Thus I no longer believe that reality is cumulative. On the view maintained in the Gifford Lectures, propositions about the past are true if there was at the time available evidence in favour of them; but propositions about the future are not reckoned true if and only if at the time to which they relate there *will be* available evidence in favour of them. On the contrary, they may be true or false now if there is conclusive reason to judge them true or false; but, if not, they will lack present truth-value, and will *become* true or false only when the time is reached to which they relate. In general, a proposition *becomes* true, and therefore comes to state a fact, only when evidence for its truth becomes available to us. In the Gifford Lectures I excused myself for treating the truth of propositions about the past and about the future asymmetrically on the ground that the view that propositions about the past are now true, if they are true, in virtue of evidence available only in the present leads to abhorrent metaphysical conclusions, whereas the dual view about propositions about the future does not.

I now think it absurd to treat past and future asymmetrically. I now believe that a proposition, whether about the past, the future or the present, is true, timelessly, just in case someone optimally placed in time and space could have, or could have had, compelling grounds for recognizing it as true—that is to say, if such compelling evidence would be or have been available to him. I hope that in the Dewey Lectures I gave more positive reasons for adopting my current view than just the need to avoid an unacceptable metaphysics of time.

I must emphasize that, on a justificationist view, there *may be* gaps in reality, but we cannot *know* that there are. If there are, then I suppose that *God* must know that there are, and then, presumably, the divine logic is, as I suggested, a three-valued rather than an intuitionist one. If there are no such gaps, so that every intelligible question has an answer, then the divine logic is classical. That seems to me a satisfying conclusion: classical logicians reason as if they were God; they are therefore guilty of overweening presumption. I must also emphasize that, even if there are no gaps, questions such as 'Is this distance exactly $3\pi/4$ metres?' do *not* have an answer; such a question is not intelligible.

My revision of the lectures has indeed been light. There were originally four lectures; I cannot remember whether I gave a supernumerary one. If I did not, I cannot imagine how I packed so much into them. I have split all the lectures into two chapters, since it is daunting for a reader to embark on a very long chapter. I think that I must at some stage have expanded the lectures, though I do not now remember doing so.

I owe thanks for helpful comments to whoever read the manuscript for the publishers. Double quotation marks are used for two purposes: as quotation marks within quotation marks; and as Quinean quasi-quotes.

Michael Dummett

Oxford
11 July 2005

Contents

I

Facts and Propositions

THE fundamental question that metaphysics strives to answer is 'What is there?', or, expressed more sententiously, 'Of what does reality consist?' Of course, metaphysics aims at an answer to this question only in the most general possible terms; but what are the most general possible terms? We might be tempted to answer, 'They are those that demand no empirical enquiry, no observation of the world, to say what there is'. But does this really mean that the metaphysician may ignore everything that natural science—even physics, the most general of the sciences—has to say about reality? Consider one who is impressed by the view expressed by C. D. Broad in his *Scientific Thought*, that not only the present but also the past exist, but that the future (so long as it *is* the future) does not. Hence at every instant a new layer is added to the sum total of reality, a temporal cross section of the world. There, without question, is a metaphysical thesis; although we may disagree with it, we can understand the process of thought that leads to its assertion. Now is it out of order to object that such a thesis violates the special theory of relativity, in that it assumes that the present moment defines a unique spacelike cross section of the universe, and thus that simultaneity is an absolute relation between events? Why should such an objection be out of order? We are trying to determine how things are; what is the use of advancing philosophical theories that must be false if generally accepted physical theories are true?

So should we say that the general terms in which metaphysics seeks to characterize reality are those that respect *necessary* features of the world, as revealed by science, but can ignore contingent ones? That simultaneity is relative to a frame of reference is intrinsic to the structure of space and time: it is not something that merely happens to be so but might not have been. It is only in the epistemic sense that we can say that it might have been absolute: that sense in which 'it might have been that . . .' means 'for all we knew at such-and-such a time, it could have turned out that . . .'. So it is *metaphysical* necessity with which we are concerned.

What are called 'metaphysical' necessity and possibility are contrasted with the epistemic varieties. They depend not upon what we know at some given time, but on the nature of what we are speaking of; they would better have been called 'ontological' necessity and possibility. But what of the nature of things may we invoke in ascribing metaphysical or ontological necessity? Might there have been centaurs? Surely not, because vertebrates all have four (actual, modified, or vestigial) limbs, whereas centaurs have six. Is it contrary to the nature of vertebrates to have six limbs? How is such a question to be decided? We have no clear insight into what is metaphysically possible. Certainly there is a distinction between uses of 'might be' and 'might have been' to express what is epistemically and what is ontologically possible; but, when these modal expressions are used in the second way, it is only from the context and from what else the speaker says that we gather what is to be taken as given. There is no determinate principle that governs what possible worlds we are to take as existing. Fortunately, there has been little or no dissension between metaphysicians over which scientific facts it is proper for them to take into consideration.

In order to say what reality consists of, it does not suffice to say what kinds of *object* there are in the world, and what constitutes the existence of such objects: it is necessary to say what kinds of *fact* obtain, and what constitutes their holding good. As Wittgenstein famously observed in the *Tractatus Logico-philosophicus*, 'The world is the totality of facts, not of things'.

How can we decide, even in the most general terms, what facts there are? What do we know about facts? One thing we know about facts, namely that we can *state* them. Whenever we make a true statement, we state some fact. To make a statement is to utter a sentence such that the utterance may be appropriately described as true or as false; it does not matter whether it would be *correctly* described as one or as the other, only that it would be in place to respond 'That is true', or 'That is false', as it would be out of place so to respond to someone's saying 'Can you lend me an umbrella?' or 'How many students are there at St Andrews?' So facts correspond to true statements: when we know which statements, in general, are true, we shall know what facts there are in general.

We are engaged in trying to clarify the fundamental question of metaphysics, not, so far, to answer it. We have not yet attained our goal, however. No philosopher has proposed to *identify* facts with true statements, largely because there is no agreement about what sort of thing a statement is, and little urge to reach any such agreement. Statements are best thought of as linguistic entities, say as declarative sentences together with assignments of references to the indexical and demonstrative expressions contained in them, or as such sentences indexed by a speaker and a time (whether or not that speaker in fact uttered that sentence at that time). So conceived, statements are made in particular languages, whereas a fact may be stated in many languages; this unfits true statements to be what facts are.

This consideration makes it more appropriate to identify facts with true *propositions*, where the term 'proposition' is understood as applying, not to declarative sentences, but to what such sentences *express*. A proposition, so understood, is not in any particular language: the same proposition may be expressed in many different languages, and in different ways in the same language. Those philosophers who are willing to use the word 'proposition' in this sense are virtually unanimous that facts are true propositions. But propositions are very slippery philosophical entities: in contrast to statements, philosophers who find the concept of a proposition useful have been very anxious to express opinions about what sort of thing a proposition is, and these opinions have been very various.

What, then, is the difference between a statement and a proposition, or between making a statement and expressing a proposition? One difference can be immediately drawn. To make a statement is to commit yourself to something, that is, to *assert* something; but you can express a proposition without committing yourself to its truth, or to anything at all. A proposition is expressed whenever a sentence is uttered whose content it is; but the sentence does not have to be uttered with what Frege called 'assertoric force'. If, when someone fails to arrive, you say, 'Either his train is late or he missed it', you have not asserted that the train was late; but you have expressed the proposition that the train was late. In this case, although you did not assert that proposition, you have asserted something, namely that one or other mishap occurred. But suppose that you are listening to a philosophical lecture, and the lecturer says, 'Change is an illusion'. You repeat to yourself the sentence 'Change is an illusion', pondering on it but not assenting to it. Now you have expressed the proposition that change is an illusion, but not in the course of asserting anything.

Philosophers have held very various views about the kind of thing a proposition is, and hence, given that facts are true propositions, about the kind of thing a fact is. Some, such as Bertrand Russell, have thought that the objects to which a proposition relates—those that are mentioned in a sentence whose utterance expresses that proposition—are actual components of the proposition; others have vehemently denied this. Philosophers of the former inclination have tended to take propositions, at least when they are true and thereby constitute facts, to be constituents of external reality, as are the objects that are components of them; philosophers of the opposite inclination have regarded propositions, not indeed as not being comprised in reality, but as denizens of a quite particular sector of it. A philosopher of this second tendency was Frege, who spoke, not of propositions, but of thoughts, which, however, he denied to be among the contents of anyone's mind: we grasp thoughts, but they are external to us, rather than being within our minds as are our mental images. For Frege, thoughts belong to a special realm of reality, which he called the 'realm of sense' and distinguished from the 'realm of reference'. The realm of reference contains what our thoughts relate to and what renders them true or false: everything we can talk or think about. Between the senses of the words composing an utterance, which combine to form the thought it expresses, and the references of those words there is, for Frege, an absolute distinction. It cannot be so between the *realm* of sense and the *realm* of reference, since, after all, we can talk about the senses of words and the thoughts expressed by sentences; so the realm of sense must be a sector of the realm of reference. But, when we talk about the senses of words, we do not *express* those senses; rather, we *refer* to them, and we may do so by using words that express quite different senses. Pythagoras's theorem is a proposition—a thought in Frege's terminology. But the words 'Pythagoras's theorem' do not *express* that thought; they only serve to name it.

In the face of such disparate opinions about what facts and propositions are, the identification of facts with true propositions appears at first sight to be of little help to our metaphysical enquiry. But reflection suggests that this is not so. We were not primarily concerned to discover what sort of thing a fact is, but, rather, what facts, in general, there are. Even if we are unsure whether propositions contain the objects to which they relate, or whether they are constituents of reality, we have taken a small step along our path when we have reduced our question to the problem what true propositions, in general, there are. Indeed, for this purpose we do not need to know whether facts *are* true propositions: it is enough to know that at least they correspond one to one with true propositions.

It often happens in philosophy that, as we proceed along a line of enquiry, we come upon a steep and muddy declivity. We may decide to jump across it, and proceed on our main path; but we may alternatively allow ourselves to slither to the bottom of the trench, clambering up out of it again before we resume our progress. So it is with the present enquiry. Even though what we want to know is what facts there are, in general, can we really ignore the problem about the nature of facts—their ontological status, to employ philosophers' jargon? For a question faces us that we can hardly evade. It is this. If facts are *not* constituents of reality, there is no problem. But if facts *are* constituents of reality, must we not include the fact that constituents of this kind exist among the facts that go to characterize reality? This question might be answered, 'No: because facts do not *exist*, they *obtain*'. But the answer appears a sophism. Among the many facts that obtain is the fact that Edinburgh is more populous than St Andrews: and how could such a fact obtain, or be known to anyone, if there were no such fact? To say that there are binary stars is to say that binary stars exist; so likewise to say that there is such-and-such a fact is to say that that fact exists. A fact cannot obtain unless it exists, and it cannot exist unless it obtains: it is no more than idiom in accordance with which we express the existence of facts by saying that they obtain.

But, now, is it correct to regard the existence of facts as a fact *additional* to those facts themselves? Surely this is a reduplication. Is there an extra fact, beyond the fact, say, that China is a Communist state, namely that that fact exists or obtains? Is not there being such a fact as that China is a Communist state the very *same* fact as the fact that China is a Communist state? After all, Wittgenstein did not say merely that reality is *determined* by what facts there are, which is undoubtedly so, but that reality—the world—is *composed* of facts. On this view, it is not that external reality contains, besides a bird perched on a bough, the fact that a bird is perched on a bough:

rather, what it contains is a bird's being perched on a bough, and that *is* the fact in question.

This conception is at first sight attractive. The world is composed not of bare *objects*, but of objects situated in relation to one another, that is, of complexes of objects such as the bird perched on the bough; and these are what we call facts, which render our statements true or false. But second thoughts bring the conception into conflict with the *generality* of facts. What complex of objects in the external world constitutes the fact that there is no bird on some particular bough, and how is it to be distinguished from the complex that constitutes the fact that there is neither a bird nor a squirrel on that bough? What complex consists in there never having been a different bird on the bough from the one that is there now? The fact that a bird is perched on a bough of the ash tree is surely a different fact from the fact that a starling is perched on a bough of the tree, since one may know the one and not the other—unless, indeed, facts are not what we know (nor propositions what we believe). Hence neither can be the same fact as that a bird is perched on a bough of the tree; and yet, given that all these *are* facts, and that the same bough of the same tree is involved in each, what different complexes existing in the world, and containing bird, tree, and bough as components, can constitute these three different facts?

Considerations of this kind drive us towards revising the conception so as to regard the world as composed only of *atomic* facts, as Wittgenstein held in the *Tractatus*. Complex facts, of whatever degree of generality, are, on this view, mere truth-functional compounds of atomic facts, and do not go to make up reality.

The seeming impossibility of identifying the atomic propositions whose truth or falsity would constitute the atomic facts that make up the world has blocked this route of escape from the dilemma: it was, indeed, this difficulty that persuaded Wittgenstein to abandon the views he had propounded in the *Tractatus*. We can, of course, distinguish between the atomic and the complex *sentences* of any given language: the atomic ones are those that do not overtly contain any logical operators. But this distinction depends heavily upon the vocabulary that the language happens to possess: it does not serve to distinguish atomic *propositions* from complex ones. An atomic proposition should be expressed by an atomic sentence that contains no expression that is not conceptually complex, that is, no expression that can be defined in terms of expressions that could be understood in advance of it; but definability depends to a notable extent upon the accident of the order in which expressions are introduced. Should we treat the adjective 'straight' as conceptually complex because it can be defined as 'neither curved nor crooked' or as 'forming a shortest path between its end-points'? Or is 'straight' conceptually simple, and 'crooked' conceptually complex? Is 'smooth' simple, and 'rough', as meaning 'not smooth', complex? Or is it the other way about? Are 'boy' and 'girl' complex, being definable as 'male child' and 'female child' respectively? Or is 'child' complex, being definable as 'boy or girl'? Obviously, these questions have no answers: there is no valid notion of a simple proposition.

It seems, therefore, that the conception of facts as constituents of external reality must be abandoned. How shall we fare if we adopt the alternative view of Frege, according to which facts, though genuine entities, inhabit a quite special sector of reality?

Frege's third realm, the realm of sense, contains, along with their component senses, propositions or thoughts regardless of whether they are true or false. They are rendered true or false by the way things are in the realm of reference—whatever sector of reality they happen to be about. On Frege's view, any adequate account of the nature of reality as a whole must acknowledge the existence of this third realm and of its denizens. But does not this picture involve the same reduplication as before? Can we not argue as before that the existence of the fact that China is a Communist state is the same fact as the fact that China is a Communist state, and that therefore the existence of the fact ought not to be listed as a fact about the world alongside the fact itself? The argument does not, this time, carry the same weight as before. On Frege's conception, the existence of the *thought* (proposition) that China is a Communist state is indeed a fact to be listed alongside the fact that China is a Communist state; but the existence of the thought is not tantamount to its truth—there are false thoughts as well as true ones. The *truth* of the thought, by contrast, is not to be listed alongside the fact about China. It just *is* the fact—facts are true thoughts; the thought that it is true that China is a Communist state is the very same thought as the thought that China is a Communist state.

Thinking or saying that a thought is true does not make it true; it is merely to entertain or express that very thought. The truth of a thought remains extraneous to it, on Frege's conception of the matter. What renders it true, if it is true, is something in the external world, the realm of reference; but its truth is not a feature of it as it is within the third realm, just as what makes Mars the fourth planet from the Sun is nothing intrinsic to Mars itself, but the existence and orbits of Mercury, Venus, and the Earth, and there being no other planet with an orbit closer to the Sun than that of Mars. The Fregean conception does not create the dilemma on which we were impaled under the Russellian or Wittgensteinian conception.

But *are* propositions (Fregean thoughts) constituents of reality at all? Do they inhabit a special immaterial sector of reality, independently of whether we grasp or entertain them, judge them to be true or false? To think of them as doing so tempts us to regard them, and the senses of our words and phrases, as constituting intermediate stations between our utterances and the constituents of the external world of which we speak: we aim at those senses, which then send us on to their associated referents in the physical world. But this picture is fallacious. It ignores the difference between *referring* to something, which we do by using an expression whose sense determines that reference, and *expressing* a sense or thought. Given the picture of a two-stage journey from utterance to component of external reality, what could this difference be? How could we pick out, in thought or speech, one proposition from others within the third realm otherwise than by referring to it, as we pick out one woman from others by referring to her? The picture is erroneous in treating the sense as a half-way station. Any feature of our use or our understanding of our words that goes to determine their reference is a component of their sense. The sense is not a station along the route: it is the route.

This is not to deny that we can refer to thoughts and their component senses as well as express them, and that they are therefore objects in the sense of being possible objects of reference. Their being is, however, to be grasped and expressed and thereby communicated. The need thus arises to explain how, in any given language, sentences express thoughts: how we grasp what thought is expressed by a sentence we hear or read, how we know how to frame a sentence to express a thought we wish to convey. Plainly, this depends on there being systematic principles that govern the expression of complex senses, and ultimately that of whole thoughts by sentences; principles that we follow though we are far from possessing a fully explicit formulation of them. Frege was the first to construct a plausible theory of such principles—a theory of meaning, that is, a theory of how a human language functions. If we have a satisfactory such theory, we have all the explanation of sense that is needed. Frege believed that he needed to postulate the third realm in order to safeguard the objectivity of thoughts and their accessibility to different individuals; but, as Wittgenstein taught us, these things are sufficiently secured by the fact that the use of a language is a common practice in which its many speakers have learned to engage.

For Frege, in his later years, reality was divided into three realms. The first was the external physical world that we all inhabit; the second comprised the inner worlds of sensations and mental images that each of us has and can only imperfectly communicate to others; and the third was the third realm of thoughts and their component senses that we can all grasp and communicate to one another by means of language. (In an earlier phase Frege would probably have added the world of arithmetic, inhabited by objective abstract objects such as cardinal numbers and the real and complex numbers.) Frege was impressed by the objectivity of thoughts, which he believed we human beings could grasp only as expressed in words or symbols: not only can they be completely communicated by one person to another, but they can be expressed in different languages. It is indeed an important fact that different languages can be translated one from another, as games cannot. It makes no sense to ask what kind of chess move corresponds to a finesse in bridge; but we readily ask, 'What is the Hungarian (Farsi, Tamil) for "soap"?' Games have no purpose beyond themselves; languages are instruments. It is natural to conclude from this, with Frege, that the propositions they serve to express subsist independently of the particular means by which we express them.

This does not follow, however; the common structure of correct theories of meaning for individual languages shows why languages must be intertranslatable. We have rejected the idea that external reality is composed of facts, that is, of true propositions. We have also rejected belief in Frege's third realm, but may still take facts to be true propositions. Propositions are not objects discovered in external reality, either material or immaterial; they are entities abstracted from the practice of using language in which all human beings engage. The phrase 'abstracted from' does not refer to the mental process of abstraction by disregarding features of concrete objects in which so many philosophers and mathematicians of the nineteenth century believed; it is indeed a process of concept-formation, but a logical rather than a mental process. It is akin to the act of forming equivalence classes familiar in mathematics, but it need not be identified with it.

All philosophers willing to use the term 'proposition' agree that the same proposition can be expressed in different ways, in particular in different languages. Since facts are true propositions, the way in which the propositions expressed by different utterances are identified or distinguished bears upon the character of the facts they state when they are true. According to Arthur Prior, a sentence such as 'It is raining in St Andrews' expresses the *same* proposition whenever it is uttered. Since such an utterance would be true at one time and false at another, Prior's view implies that a proposition may be true at certain times and false at others; correspondingly, a fact may obtain at a certain time, and later fail to obtain, and later still come to obtain again. Frege held, on the contrary, that what he called a thought must be true or false absolutely, irrespective of when or by whom it is expressed: it follows that the sentence 'It is raining in St Andrews' expresses a different thought or proposition according to the time at which it is uttered. Because the notion of a proposition is linked to metaphysics in virtue of the identification of facts with true propositions, the disagreement between Prior and Frege is not merely one about logic: it is a disagreement about the character of reality itself. Does it comprise evanescent or discontinuous states of affairs? Or is it of itself unchanging, most faithfully described by propositions stating eternal facts that subsist indifferently to the passage of time?

There are two separable questions here. Frege held that what thought is expressed by a sentence whose only temporal indicator was indexical (such as the tense of the verb or an adverb like 'tomorrow') depended on the time it was uttered; Prior thought it merely had the effect that the proposition expressed had a truth-value that varied with time. This is the first question. The second is how we should construe temporal indicators, whether indexical or otherwise. Do they occupy argument-places tacitly carried by the predicates of sentences reporting events or variable states of affairs? Or, as Davidson would have it, predicates applying to a bound variable ranging over events and states of affairs? Or are they operators, as Prior believed? The first question expressly concerns which utterances express the same proposition. If we deny that the time of utterance goes to determine the proposition expressed, we have no option but to take the sentence 'It is raining in St Andrews' as expressing the *same* proposition whenever it is uttered. But the second question does not mention propositions. If we treat temporal indicators as operators, analogous to modal operators, we must ask what they operate on. The answer must be that they operate on sentences in the present tense, that tense being treated as timeless except when no temporal indicator is present. 'It will rain in St Andrews tomorrow' will be construed as 'It will be the case tomorrow that it is raining in St Andrews'. Sentences in the present tense are thus the units to which our sentential operators are applied. But there will be no need to regard such units as expressing the same proposition whenever uttered (at least if they contain no locative or personal indexicals such as 'here' and 'I'). We can still, if we wish, follow Frege in taking the time of utterance as contributing to fixing what proposition is expressed.

2

Semantics and Metaphysics

WHAT is to decide issues such as the logical category of temporal indicators—whether they are arguments of many-place predicates or sentential operators? The decision will determine the shape of the semantic theory that we adopt: the theory that explains how statements are determined as true or as false in terms of their composition out of their constituent expressions. But it also bears upon the metaphysics we accept—our conception of the constitution of reality. For Prior, reality is mutable. It contains facts that hold good at one time and cease to hold good at a later time. Which depends on which—the semantics on the metaphysics or the metaphysics on the semantics? Do we first have to make up our minds about the metaphysical question, and then shape our semantics in accordance with the answer? This is the strategy that philosophers have frequently followed; but it is a misguided one. It is misguided because we then have no way of deciding the metaphysical question. By what means can we determine the general character of reality without adverting to the character of the propositions we take as holding good of reality?

We do have a means of settling the question what semantic theory to adopt, on the other hand, without appeal to any prior metaphysical judgement. For a semantic theory, to be acceptable, must pass a number of diverse tests. First, it must be a coherent theory in itself; and, in so complex a matter, this test is not negligible. Secondly, it must, at least by and large, deliver the *right* truth-conditions for our statements, those which, in virtue of our understanding of our language, we acknowledge as the conditions under which those statements would in fact be correct. Thirdly, it must make possible a plausible explanation of what it is in which a speaker's understanding of the words, phrases, and sentences of his language consists. To understand an expression is to know what it means, that is, to grasp its meaning. A semantic theory purports to explain what it is for expressions of the language to have the meanings that they do. It should therefore render it possible to say what constitutes someone's grasping those meanings; if it fails to provide for such an account, or delivers an account that is not credible, it has failed one of the central tasks of a semantic theory. And, fourthly, given the account of understanding that can be constructed on the basis of that semantic theory, it must be comprehensible how we could come to acquire such an understanding of our language. These are stiff tests to pass, and ones for which it is far from obvious at a glance whether or not a given semantic theory passes them.

Our metaphysics is therefore to be determined by our semantic theory. In any semantic theory, linguistic items of some particular kind will be treated by the theory as its *basic units*. These will necessarily be type sentences, whether of a natural language or of such a language regimented by having its sentences put into a standardized form suitable for logical manipulation. There is a strong inclination to identify the basic units, either in themselves as type sentences or as uttered on particular hypothetical or actual occasions, as what express propositions. Sentences, for the purposes of any given semantic theory, will be whatever that theory selects as its basic units. It will assign to the basic units *semantic values* of a particular kind in terms of which the semantic values of all sub-sentential expressions that go to make up the sentences or basic units will be defined: their values will consist of their contributions to determining the semantic values of any basic units of which they are constituents and of nothing irrelevant to making such contributions. The theory will explain how the semantic values of the constituents of a basic unit combine to fix the semantic value of the whole; it will thus effectively show how the meanings of sentences are determined by their composition. The basic units will be divided into atomic ones, involving no logical operators in their composition, and complex ones involving them. The basic units will therefore also be those linguistic items, whether atomic or already complex, to which the logical operations are applied; it is such logical operations that enable us to form complex sentences out of simpler ones.

These operations are, first, the sentential operations of negation, conjunction, disjunction, and conditionalization, together with whatever others, such as the modalizations expressed by 'must' and 'may', for which the semantic theory allows. The second type of logical operation is, of course, quantification, by means of which generality is expressed. Thus Prior took type sentences in the present tense as his basic units, because he viewed the past and future tenses, and other means of specifying times, as sentential operators, arguing that only in this way could complex tenses such as the future perfect ('will have') and the past future ('was going to') be accommodated. He assumed that the basic units must be what expressed propositions, leading to the conclusion that such a sentence as 'It is raining in St Andrews' must express the same proposition whenever it is uttered. But we have seen that this conclusion does not follow. That temporal reference is effected by sentential operators in no way implies that the time of reference is irrelevant to the proposition expressed. (Unless our modal logic is S5, the analogue fails for modal statements.) Whether 'tomorrow' is an argument, a predicate, or an operator, we are free to consider that which proposition was expressed by the utterance of a sentence containing it depends upon the day on which the sentence was uttered.

What is the importance of deciding when two utterances express the same proposition? We have seen that our metaphysics is to be determined by our semantic theory. But the present question does not depend upon our semantic theory. The concept of truth belongs to semantics, since after all truth is what must be preserved by a valid deductive inference. But the concept of a proposition does not belong to semantics. Semantics determines whether or not two sentences express the same sense; it also determines which expressions are indexical. But it has no need to operate with the concept of a proposition. This appears to weaken, if not sever, the link between semantics and metaphysics: if the world is the totality of facts, and facts are true propositions, then what has a theory that does not employ the concept of a proposition to do with the structure of reality?

A semantic theory applies to just one language. But the features of the theory, if it is correct, that have metaphysical implications are the general ones that must be shared with a correct semantic theory for any other language. Thus every language must have some means of indicating when an event being narrated occurred, or when any state of affairs being reported obtained; so a proposal for how temporal indicators are to be construed must apply to semantic theories for all languages. If humanity had only one language (as before Babel), it would suffice to say that reality was determined by which statements were true; it would not matter that different statements may express the same proposition. To substitute 'propositions' for 'statements' acknowledges that there are many languages, but that the structure of reality does not depend on which of them we consider. The word 'proposition' is a term of art; but we employ the concept in everyday speech. Suppose that Philip says to me 'I am afraid Bertram does not like you'; I may reply 'I said the same thing yesterday', when what I then said was 'Bertram ne m'aime pas'. Admittedly, we may use the phrase 'the same thing' in a different sense; if I say today 'There will be a thunderstorm this evening', Philip may reply 'You said the same thing yesterday', when what I said yesterday was 'There will be a thunderstorm this evening'. For Prior, I *did* express the same proposition yesterday as I expressed today. Is there a truth of the matter whether he was right to think this?

There is not. We want propositions to be what are expressed by utterances of declarative sentences, but are expressible in different languages and by different sentences in the same language. They may be true or false, and we may take facts to be true propositions. If reality is to be determined by what facts there are, it is inconvenient to think of facts as flickering in and out of existence, now obtaining and now no longer obtaining; so the more useful concept of a proposition is as dependent on the time of utterance. Whether change occurs *in* reality or whether reality itself changes can be discussed independently of whether we identify propositions as Prior did or as Frege identified thoughts.

This is an undeniably metaphysical question. If it does not turn on whether the time of utterance goes to determine what proposition is expressed, to what semantic disagreement is it related? Plainly, change occurs *in* reality; any occasion on which it is true to say 'It is much colder than it was yesterday' is witness to that, if witness were needed.

But does reality itself change? What can be meant by this? It would seem to be true if *presentism* is correct—the doctrine that there *is* nothing, nothing at all, save what holds good at the present moment. But the present changes, second by second; for instance, in the past second the bird in the garden stopped singing, and the light emitted by a supernova in some distant galaxy is now one light-second closer to us. And so, on the presentist view, as the present changes, so reality changes with it.

Or is this the presentist view? If presentism were correct, there would not, now, be any past or any future, and so nothing in virtue of which what we say or think about what has happened or what will happen would be true or false. And if that is so, we cannot even say that the present changes, because that requires that things are not now as they were some time ago.

The presentist may retort that statements about the past and the future, understood in accordance with their real meanings, are rendered true or false only by what lies in the present—our memories and what we treat as traces of the past, and present tendencies towards some outcome. If this is what is meant by saying how things were yesterday, or one second ago, then indeed the present, and with it reality, changes.

We may say that the presentist is wrong: statements about the past or the future are *not* rendered true or false by what lies in the present. And now it is very clear what semantic disagreement underlies the metaphysical one. We did not need to invoke the notion of a proposition in order to bring it out: the notions of truth and falsity were sufficient. The thesis that reality changes could of course be maintained on other than presentist grounds: for instance, it might be maintained that the whole of spacetime, with all that it contains, permanently exists, but that a moving beam of actuality steadily advances across a temporal cross section of it. But this, too, and all other variations, would have a semantic substrate.

Thus, presentism would necessarily require a semantics that repudiated the principle of bivalence: if statements about the past and about the future are to be evaluated as true or as false on the basis solely of present evidence and present indications, there can be no guarantee that there will be grounds to judge an arbitrary statement of either kind to possess one or the other truth-value. An adherent of the second conception, that of the beam of actuality, would naturally accept bivalence for statements void of indexical expressions (including significantly tensed verbs), and apply a truth-conditional semantics to such statements. He will probably treat sentences containing indexical expressions as making statements that are likewise determinately either true or false on any occasion when they are uttered; the reference of the indexical expressions will be fixed according to the identity of the speaker and the time at which the utterance was actual. Both these two standpoints conflict with special relativity in the way mentioned in Chapter 1, in that they assume simultaneity to be absolute. But they serve to illustrate how different metaphysical conceptions are reflected by different semantic theories, and, more generally, theories of meaning.

But how can it be reasonable to base our metaphysics on our semantics? How can we arrive at the right conception of the reality of which we speak, but which we take to exist independently of us and of what we say about it, by studying the structure of the language by means of which we speak of it? What can mere *language* have to do with reality?

The answer depends upon just how mere we take language to be. There are two opposing philosophical views concerning the relative priority, in the order of explanation and even of acquisition, of thought and language. According to one school, which we may call the linguistic school, our attainment of the capacity to grasp and entertain thoughts, at least of thoughts of any but a quite low level of complexity, runs in parallel with our attainment of the ability to express those thoughts in language: it is *by* learning to express and communicate them that we come to apprehend the thoughts we so express. A more moderate version of the 'linguistic' view remains agnostic about the order in which we acquire these abilities, but agrees that the ability to grasp thoughts *could* be acquired by learning to express those thoughts without previously having been able to entertain them, and holds that the only feasible means of achieving an account of the structure of our thoughts and of our grasp of them lies in an analysis of the structure of the sentences of our language and of their power of expression without presupposing what it is to grasp the thoughts that they express.

The opposing school, which comprises what may be called 'philosophers of thought', maintains that it is in principle possible for those devoid of language to entertain the thoughts that we have and to grasp the concepts that we grasp, and that it is likewise in principle possible to give a philosophical account of the structure of those thoughts and of what constitutes a grasp of them without adverting to the means of expressing them linguistically. For these philosophers of thought, accordingly, a theory of linguistic meaning may legitimately presuppose a grasp, on the part of the speakers of the language, of the thoughts and concepts expressible in it, and, as an assumption of the theory, a philosophical understanding of what it is to grasp those thoughts and concepts: the construction of a theory of meaning is thus for them at once an easier and a less important task than it is for linguistic philosophers. The view of the philosophers of thought was adumbrated by Frege when he wrote that there is no inconsistency in supposing beings capable of grasping the same thoughts as ourselves without needing to clothe them in words or symbols; he was, however, emphatic that *we* are not such beings.

In this dispute, I am myself strongly on the side of the linguistic school, and shall later in this chapter explain one of my reasons for being so. For our immediate purposes, however, it matters little which of the two schools is in the right. The philosophy of thought stands in need of a theory that occupies the place in it that is occupied by a semantic theory in a philosophical account of how language functions. Just as sentences have structure, being composed of words that themselves combine to form substructures, so thoughts have structure, being formed out of concepts that themselves combine to form component conceptual complexes. A philosophy of thought must explain what it is for a thought to have the content that it does, just as a theory of meaning must explain what it is for a sentence to have the meaning that it does; and it must explain how that content is determined by the internal structure of the thought out of its component concepts. This may be termed the structural section of a philosophy of thought; and most of what I said about semantic theories will hold good of such a structural section. It, too, must recognize thoughts of a certain general type as its basic theoretical units; it, too, must distinguish, among them, between atomic ones and complex ones. For present purposes, we need not decide whether thought or language has the priority in the order of explanation.

This reply will satisfy those perturbed simply by a salient role's being accorded to *language* in the quest for the general character of reality; it will not satisfy those perturbed by such a role's being accorded to human thought, whether or not expressed in language. Why should we suppose that we can reach any valid conclusions about the nature of reality itself by consideration of what *we* are capable of thinking about it? Surely reality must be a far more extensive thing than the narrow and no doubt distorted picture that we can form of it. This is a false opposition. We can compare a picture of something with that which it represents, and judge how faithful the representation is; but we are not then comparing a picture with a picture, that is, a mental picture of the physical picture with a mental picture of what the physical picture represents. According to the latter conception, we are eternally enclosed in a world of pictures, and can never encounter the reality of which they are pictures; but, if this were in truth our lot, we should have no right to speak of any such reality, and could make no sense of speaking of it, since we could form no conception of it and should have no means of discovering anything about it if we were able to conceive it. If we misrepresent reality as we apprehend it as no more than a picture, then the reality as it is in itself of which we take ourselves to have only a picture is a conception projected solely by analogy: it must be to reality as we apprehend it as a real landscape is to a painted landscape. We know what it is to view a real landscape; but a reality that we can never apprehend, because any apprehension of it will necessarily be no more than a picture, is a phantasm produced by pushing analogy beyond its legitimate limits.

This is not, of course, to deny that we are constantly engaged in an effort to correct our beliefs about the world. The sciences, history, and philosophy, in fact all types of intellectual endeavour, participate in this process; over the centuries, our progress has been very substantial. We replace false thoughts by true thoughts, or at least by thoughts that make a closer approach to truth; false beliefs by knowledge, or at least by less erroneous beliefs: but what we are left with are still thoughts that, at any rate for the time being, we judge to be true. The world, in so far as we apprehend it and are capable of coming to apprehend it, is the world we inhabit; of what we are incapable of apprehending we cannot meaningfully speak. In asking after the character of reality, we are asking after that of the world we inhabit; to speak of a world transcending ours and, as it were, encasing it, is merely to employ a form of words devoid of any clear sense. Reality is constituted by what facts there are, and the notion of a fact is one that *we* have framed. The only facts of which we can conceive are those that render our beliefs, and other beliefs that we may come to form, true or false. Hence to enquire what facts there are is to enquire what thoughts that we can grasp are true: not just the thoughts we now grasp, but those that we have the capacity to grasp and may later grasp. The contribution that metaphysics can make to answering this question is on the highest level of generality: it has to do with the nature of propositions and with what constitutes their truth. Other forms of intellectual enquiry seek to determine *which* propositions are true. Metaphysics seeks to determine what it is for them to be true. The only means by which it can do this is to unravel the nature of propositions—of the thoughts we are capable of thinking.

In the processes of everyday life, including the processes of intellectual discovery, for those engaged upon them, we know how to operate with our language and hence with the thoughts we use it to express. But we are like soldiers in a battle, who know what they have to do, but have no idea what in general is going on: we do not command a clear view of the working of our language or of the full content of our thoughts. It is such a clear view for which philosophy strives, stumblingly and following many false leads.

Propositions are grasped by processes of thought and expressed in language. But may there not be aspects of reality that lie beyond our power to grasp or express? May there not be propositions, and true propositions among them, facts therefore, that our language is incapable of expressing and our minds incapable of grasping? There are surely propositions that we are *now* incapable of grasping or of expressing. For there are propositions that we can now grasp and express, but that at earlier times in our history we not only neither grasped nor expressed, but *could not* then either grasp or express, because they involve concepts that we did not then have, but that were only later introduced, conveyed, and explained. The process by which an expression for a genuinely new concept is introduced—one that cannot be straightforwardly defined in terms of concepts we already possess—is a puzzling one, that deserves detailed study; but it can hardly be denied that there is such a process. New concepts are explained linguistically, but by means that fall short of being definitions; they could not have been expressed, however circuitously, in the language as it was before the explanation was given.

In this sense, therefore, a denial that there are propositions, and hence also facts, that we cannot now grasp or express would be unjustifiable. By the same token, it would be unjustified to deny that there are propositions, and hence also facts, that we shall *never* grasp or be able to express: for there is no reason to claim that we shall sooner or later grasp every concept that we are in principle capable of grasping, and should grasp if it were properly explained to us. A language may be regarded as embracing everything that can be expressed in it, including what could be perspicuously expressed only by means of new terms definable by expressions already in the language. An extended conception would take it as embracing whatever could be expressed by means of terms that were capable of being explained, though not properly speaking defined, by the use of the language as now constituted. We must count as a proposition anything that is expressible, in this extended sense, in the language that we use.

But may it not be that there are propositions, and hence facts about the world, that we are in principle, as human beings with the mental capacities to which human beings, even at their best, are restricted, for ever incapable of grasping, and therefore of expressing? If there are, we cannot of course ever give the slightest indication of what these might be: but would it not be arrogant and presumptuous to rule out the possibility of their existence? What we cannot say we cannot say, and therefore we cannot think what we cannot say. Or better: what we cannot think we cannot think, and therefore we cannot say what we cannot think.

But is there not also the inexpressible? Yet what can it *mean* to say that there are facts that we cannot in principle express? That we are incapable even in the extended sense of expressing? What could debar us from expressing such facts? The limitations of our minds? Or the limitations of our language? It is unclear that our language *has* limitations, if we understand its scope in the extended sense. Any genuine concept must be capable of being explained, even if the explanation would require the prior explanation of other concepts at present unfamiliar to us, and would enormously extend our conceptual armoury; and, if so, our language could be expanded by means of such explanations so as to render it capable of expressing propositions involving that concept.

So perhaps it is by the limitations of our minds that we are blocked from understanding such explanations and hence grasping such a concept. It sounds very humble to speak of the limitations of our minds: but towards whom is this humility directed? Only towards *possible* other creatures, it would appear: for we are the only kind of creature of which we have any acquaintance capable of thinking at all. Perhaps this is too strong a claim: do not birds and mammals, perhaps even reptiles, have thoughts of a kind, and knowledge of a kind? We need not explore this question here: it is enough that, while such animals may be said to have a picture of their environment—which, in the case of migrating birds, may be quite extensive—they cannot be said to have, or even to seek, a picture of *the world*, that is of reality as a whole. Whether or not collective humility towards merely possible beings is genuinely a virtue, arrogance is not a logical vice: the fact that it is arrogant to maintain a certain thesis has no tendency to show that it is false, or even improbable. We are certainly ignorant of many features of reality, and we may never in fact succeed in grasping what some of them are: but no proof has been advanced to show that there are features of it that we could never in principle comprehend.

Is this not what Wittgenstein was propounding in the *Tractatus* when he wrote, '*The limits of my language* signify the limits of my world'? Perhaps not exactly; he was concerned in that passage not with the limits of *our* world, but with those of *my* world; and, from our present standpoint, all human beings inhabit the same world. Still, cannot it be said that the limits of our language signify the limits of our world?

But perhaps it is not towards other *creatures* that our collective humility is directed. The prophet Isaiah wrote, "For my thoughts are not your thoughts, neither are your ways my ways", says the Lord. "For as the heavens are higher than the earth, so are my ways higher than your ways and my thoughts than your thoughts." Are there not thoughts that God has, and facts that God knows, that we are incapable of understanding or conceiving? Would not the arrogance of denying *this* amount to a logical error?

The whole problem is deep. For the present, let us set it aside, to take it up again in a later chapter, and turn to ask with what warrant I rejected a concern with *my* world in favour of a concern with *our* world. There is doubtless an acceptable sense in which each of us lives within his own private world. But this is not the sense of 'world' that is relevant either to what thoughts are available to any one of us or to what any one of us knows. Human beings are rational animals: and this means animals capable of a high level of thought. Observation, experiment, and speculation may enable us to form a conception of the thoughts that animals such as horses, dogs, and elephants have, and of how they achieve an ability to form them; but our ability to have the thoughts we have depends strictly upon our interaction with other human beings. It is that interaction that renders us human; without it we should lack the characteristics that distinguish rational animals from other animals, those that are manifested by our engaging in thought at a high level. Wolf children, children who have grown up in wolf society, can never make the adaptation needed to become properly human. What enables us to have the thoughts we do is our ability to express them; acquiring the ability to think as we do and acquiring a mastery of one of the many languages in which we express them and convey them to others are one and the same process. Language is essentially a communal practice, and each language has been shaped by a long historical process: we owe our ability to talk, and hence our ability to think as we do, to the other human beings who surrounded us in childhood, and ultimately to our forefathers who died long before we were born.

Consider, as an example, a very fundamental concept, that of memory. The process of acquiring this concept cannot be realistically described without reference to the use of language; indeed, it cannot be imagined otherwise. A rudimentary grasp of the use of the past tense precedes the acquisition of the concept of memory. Parents use the past tense to remark to the child on things he has just witnessed— 'The bird has flown away', 'Lucy fell over'—and then on things that happened quite recently—'Where's the lovely doll Aunt Susan gave you yesterday?': they rely on the child's remembering the events in question, without his yet knowing what it is to remember something. With the past tense in his stock of forms of expression, the child will then spontaneously come out with reports of memory; he also spontaneously comes out with reports of his dreams. The formation both of the concept of memory and of the concept of dreaming depends critically upon the different reactions the adults have to reports of these two kinds. To what is obviously the report of a dream, they react by assuring him that it did not really happen; they make clear that they are not accusing him of making it up, and *give* him the word 'dream' to use in giving such reports. But the child learns to distinguish his memory-reports from his reports of dreams as being capable of being right or wrong; he is applauded when his memory-reports are known to be correct, put right when they are known to be mistaken. He learns that they are a source of information for others, who may piece them together with facts known to them from other sources to make up a complex narrative. He learns that not all that he knows about what has happened counts as memory—for instance, not if he was told it by others: he must have witnessed the event himself for his report to constitute a memory, and thus a source of information. Without this guidance and instruction from others, he might frame some approximations to our concepts of memory and of dreaming; but they could be no more than unsubtle caricatures of the concepts we employ.

The same holds good for knowledge as for language and hence for thought. An animal without language may teach many skills to its young; it cannot teach them *facts*, though it can direct their attention to some. But how much of the knowledge that any of us has should we have if we had to discover everything we know for ourselves? Our knowledge is mostly made up of things we have read or that others have told us by word of mouth: our knowledge, and hence our picture of the world, draw heavily upon the store of knowledge commonly available. Both as thinkers and as knowers, we are utterly dependent on others of our kind: the world any one of us inhabits is not *his* world, but *our* world. We are members of society just as much as we are individuals: not more than we are individuals, but just as much.

3
Truth and Meaning

It is not only philosophers of the school that we rejected, that which holds that facts are constituents of external reality, who equate facts with true propositions: such an identification may instead express a repudiation of the conception of facts as constituents of reality. Frege, as we saw, relegated propositions, which he called 'thoughts', to a special realm, the realm of sense: thoughts, for him, were the *senses* of sentences, or, more exactly, of particular utterances of them; the sense of a particular utterance of a sentence containing such indexical expressions as 'here', 'yesterday', 'I', and so forth, or such demonstrative expressions as 'this', 'those', and the like, is determined not by the words alone, but also by the circumstances of the utterance. But he held facts to be true thoughts. This was, for him, a way of stating that facts do *not* belong to the realm of reference, that is, to whatever sector of reality we are talking about and which serves to render what we say true or false; Frege wanted to have some means of accommodating the notion of a fact, without regarding reality as composed of complexes constituting what make certain propositions true. To say that facts are true propositions, and that reality — that reality we talk about — is composed of facts, entails that external reality contains items that qualify as true. For Frege, however, it makes sense to attribute truth or falsity only to a very special kind of thing, an immaterial entity inhabiting a special realm—namely a thought. So his solution was to identify facts with true thoughts, thus allowing facts a place in his ontology—his catalogue of what there is in the world—but a place only within the realm of sense.

Those philosophers who are willing to use both the terms 'fact' and 'proposition' in philosophical discourse have thus been all but unanimous that facts are true propositions, and those who have for one or another reason dissented from so identifying them have agreed that, even if they *are* not true propositions, at any rate they *correspond to* true propositions. I earlier argued that the concept of a proposition does not belong to semantics. But the notion of the content of an utterance does belong to it, where the content is what the hearer believes if he accepts the statement uttered as true (whether or not it was propounded as such). The bridge that connects semantics to metaphysics thus rests on two pillars, the concept of *content*, so understood, and the concept of *truth*. We have paid some attention to the notion of content, as approximated by the concept of a proposition; we must now scrutinize more closely the concept of truth.

Frege wrote, 'What I have called a thought stands in the closest connection with truth'; and a thought, for him, was the *sense* of a sentence. Russell wrote a book entitled *An Inquiry into Meaning and Truth*. From Frege onwards, through Bertrand Russell and Donald Davidson down to Gareth Evans and John McDowell, most philosophers—not all, indeed—have recognized the 'closest connection' between the concepts of truth and of meaning. What is this connection? Well, how can we explain the notion of truth *except* in connection with that of meaning? Suppose that we attempt to explain truth, as an attribute of sentences or of utterances of them, without taking the meanings of those sentences as given. How can we do that? How can we say what it is for some given sentence to be true if we do not assume that we know what that sentence means? A supporter of what is frequently called a 'minimalist' account of truth has an answer to this. He replies, 'To explain what the word "true" means, you do not need to be able to say, for any given sentence S, *what it is for* S to be true; you need only to specify the significance of any other sentence, T say, that serves to attribute truth to S. And that is simply done: such a sentence T has the very same significance as S'. But suppose S lacks significance; S is, for example, the sentence 'The toves gimbled in the wabe'. 'In that case', the minimalist replies, 'T will likewise be without significance'. But T may be 'The first thing Johnson said at lunch today was quite true'; and how can that be without significance? It may be false, without doubt; since we are assuming that S *was* the first thing Johnson said at lunch, T is certainly false, since a nonsensical sentence cannot be 'quite true'; but T is perfectly meaningful, and circumstances can easily be imagined in which it would be true.

The dilemma might be escaped if the minimalist were to say, not that T has the same *significance* as S, but merely that it has the same *truth-value*. But, since S is nonsensical, it will be neither true nor false, whereas, since S is not true, T must surely be simply false: the dilemma has not been avoided after all. In any case, the modified explanation appears circular. 'Have the same truth-value' means 'either are both true or are both false'. The minimalist was, however, purporting to provide an *explanation* of the term 'true'; but the modified version explains that adjective in terms of the words 'true' and 'false'. Obviously, it is not permissible to *use* the word 'true' in explaining what the word 'true' means.

Perhaps the minimalist can wriggle out of this difficulty, and perhaps he cannot: it is not my purpose to pursue objections of this kind to minimalism. What is clear is that, for minimalists of this variety, there is no saying what it is for any given sentence to be true in advance of knowing its meaning. Once its meaning is known, then indeed we can say what it is for that sentence to be true: but, even if the meanings were given, there would still be no such thing as what it is for any arbitrary sentence to be true. The minimalist account indeed recognizes a tight connection between meaning and truth. If things in the world had been different, a sentence S (not that previously cited) would have been false, whereas, as things are, it is true: but the *condition* for its truth would be unaltered. But, if **S** had had a different meaning, the condition for it to be true would be different, and, conversely, if the condition for **S** to be true had been different, it would have had a different meaning: meaning and truth-conditions are tightly linked. Yet, on a minimalist account of truth as an attribute of sentences, the notion of truth can be of no use in explaining meaning. On such an account, you can know the condition for a sentence to be true only when you know what the sentence means; the explanation of what it means, and of what it is for it to have that meaning, must therefore be given in some manner that does not appeal to the notion of the sentence's being true.

Suppose, now, that we adopt the converse strategy, treating an explanation of the concept of truth as posterior to an account of meaning. This again implies that any account of what meaning is in general, or, in particular, of the meanings of the sentences to which we are envisaging truth as being ascribed, has been given in some manner that does not appeal to the notion of the sentences' being true, since that notion is to be explained on the assumption that we already know what meaning is and what those particular sentences mean. Any account of truth conforms to this model if it takes truth to be an attribute, not of sentences or of utterances of them, but of *propositions*. For to know what proposition the utterance of a sentence expresses is to know what that utterance means, or, at least, to know a large component of its meaning. There is a variety of such theories: classical theories of truth, such as the correspondence and coherence theories, all took truth as an attribute of propositions, and hence presupposed meanings as given in advance of the concepts of truth and falsity. To adopt the converse strategy of treating a philosophical account of meaning as antecedent to an account of the concept of truth does not necessitate taking truth to be an attribute of propositions, however: it is consistent with still taking it to be an attribute of sentences or of utterances of them, but requires us, when explaining the concept of truth, to take the meanings of the sentences to which it is applied, and an account of what it is for them to have the meanings that they do, as given.

Whether an explanation of truth arrived by following this converse strategy will represent truth and meaning as tightly connected with one another will depend upon the form that the explanation takes. What is certain is that, like explanations arrived at by means of the opposite strategy, it will require us to fashion an account of meaning that makes no appeal to the concept of truth.

A particular version of theories that treat meaning as prior to truth (in the order of explanation) is another form of minimalist theory: according to this, truth is an attribute of propositions, and is explained by the principle that an ascription of truth to any given proposition is equivalent to that very proposition. There is no difficulty for this brand of minimalism about ascribing truth to the proposition that the toves gimbled in the wabe, or to the proposition expressed by the sentence 'The toves gimbled in the wabe': there is no such proposition, and hence saying that that proposition is true is like saying that the King of France is bald.

On this version of minimalism, too, there is a tight connection between truth and meaning, in this case via a tight connection between the concept of truth and that of a proposition. But if **P** is the proposition that the British electoral system will undergo no change in the next hundred years, and **P** was the first proposition expressed by Fletcher at lunchtime, then the proposition **Q** that the first proposition expressed by Fletcher at lunchtime was true serves to ascribe truth to **P**. It is difficult to credit that **Q** is the very same proposition as **P**, however: for it is easy to imagine hypothetical circumstances in which **Q** would be false but **P** true. Just as before, the difficulty cannot be circumvented by modifying the minimalist explanation to state that an ascription of truth to any given proposition has the same truth-value as that proposition; for this would again be a circular explanation.

Others who must necessarily hold truth to be an attribute of propositions, not of sentences, are the philosophers of thought: in their case there is no presumption that meaning is given in advance of the notion of truth, for they are not concerned with linguistic entities such as sentences, nor, therefore, with their meanings. They cannot dispense with the notion of truth, however. It is essential to the propositions we judge to be correct, reject, or merely consider that they are capable of being true and of being false: no philosophy of thought could deserve serious attention unless it allowed a place for a proposition's being true and explained in what its being true consisted.

The notion that plays a role in the philosophy of thought analogous to that played by the notion of meaning in the philosophy of language is that of the content of a thought. (This notion of course differs from that of the content of a linguistic utterance.) The difference is that, while there is an obvious distinction between a sentence and its meaning, and while two different sentences, in the same or different languages, may have the same meaning, no distinction is to be drawn between a proposition and its content; no two distinct propositions can have the same content. This apart, however, there is an exact parallelism, as regards the place of the concept of truth in a correct theory, of the relevant kind, between the philosophy of language and the philosophy of thought. There are again three possible positions concerning the place of truth in the philosophy of thought. First, it may be held that truth and content must be explained together: that is, that explaining what it is for a proposition to be true and explaining what confers on a proposition the content that it has are parts of a single theory, and cannot be separated from one another. Alternatively, it may be held that the general *condition* for a proposition to be true can be formulated in advance and independently of an account of what determines a proposition's content. And, finally, it may be held that an account of content need make no appeal to the notion of truth, but may be given antecedently to an explanation of that notion. Since this parallelism obtains, we do not need, for our purposes, to pay separate attention to truth as it figures in the philosophy of thought: if we were to do so, we should only reduplicate our discussion.

The upshot of all this is that, if we attempt either to explain the concept of truth antecedently to explaining what meaning is, or to explain meaning antecedently to saying what it is for something to be true, we shall be lumbered with giving an account of meaning without appeal to the notion of truth. The same holds good if we try to explain truth using the minimalist strategy, whereby the word 'true' is reduced to a device that serves to replace the utterance of a sentence by a statement apparently about that utterance, or the expression of a proposition by one apparently about that proposition. But why should an account of meaning without appeal to the notion of truth be difficult to give? Well, it is intuitively evident that the notions of truth and meaning are closely connected to one another. If circumstances had been different, a true utterance might have been false while meaning just the same as before, and a true proposition have been false although its content remained the same. But the *condition* for the truth of the utterance could not be different without its meaning having changed, and the condition for the truth of a proposition could not be different, for it would then be a different proposition. Meaning and truth-conditions must vary together. If two people genuinely agree about all the relevant circumstances and all the relevant considerations, and agree that these are decisive, but one still judges a certain statement to be true while the other judges it to be false, they *must* be assigning different meanings to the statement. If meaning and truth have not been explained together, as part of a single complex theory, the connection between them must be accounted for, either by the way meaning is explained or by the way truth is explained; and when meaning is to be explained without appeal to the concept of truth, this is not easy to do.

What is a philosophical explanation of meaning, in the sense in which I have been using this expression? It is something very different from an everyday explanation of a word or of an utterance, of the kind that we give in answer to a question of the form 'What does this word mean?' or 'What did he mean?' We usually answer such questions by giving an equivalent expression or a sentence equivalent in the context; dictionaries do the same for almost all the words they list. Answers of this kind presuppose that the questioner understands the verb 'to mean': they do not say what constitutes the word or utterance's meaning what it does, but simply state what it is that it means. But a philosophical explanation of meaning does not presuppose a prior understanding of what meaning is: it attempts to explain what meaning is as to one ignorant of the concept. Not that a philosopher of language, in devising such an explanation, supposes his readers to lack an everyday understanding of the verb 'to mean'; he thinks only that their understanding of it is purely *implicit*, leaving them quite unable to *say* what it is for a word or sentence to have a meaning. What the philosopher of language desires—what any philosopher must desire—is to render that understanding fully explicit.

But how can we possibly say, *in general*, what it is for a word to have a meaning? It is a commonplace that words have meanings of very different kinds, contribute in very different ways to the meanings of sentences in which they occur. The most we can hope to do is to distinguish the different *types* of words, and say what it is for a word of each of these different types to have a meaning appropriate to words of that type. In doing so, we shall be forced to speak of the contribution a word of each type makes to the meaning of a sentence containing it: as Frege famously said, 'It is only in the context of a sentence that a word has a meaning'. Our task will then be to say what, in general, it is for a sentence to have a specific meaning.

Someone who is puzzled about what it is for the utterance of a sentence to have a meaning is puzzled about what language is. He has a language, and knows how to use it, but he does not know what it is that he knows in knowing that. For a sentence to have a meaning is for an utterance of it to have a certain significance; and for that to have such a significance is for it to make a difference, or at least a potential difference, to what subsequently happens, apart from the purely physical effects of those sounds. It would have no more than those purely physical effects if it were not part of a *language*; and so, to understand its significance, we must know what a language is and how speaking in that language can have the effects that it does.

A philosophical account of linguistic meaning must thus take the form of a philosophical account of language: we have to seek an explanation of what it is for something to be a language, which means an explanation of how a language functions in the lives of those who use it. A full explanation must take nothing for granted. We, who are trying to construct such an explanation, already possess a language. We are not in the position of Martians observing human beings and trying to arrive at a theory to explain the phenomena of speech and of writing and printing. We are equipped with numerous concepts that have to do with our use of language: concepts such as those of telling, saying something, talking about something, asking, answering, subject matter, denial, retraction, stating, asserting, meaning itself, and a host of others. Possessing these concepts will guide us in framing our explanation of how a language functions; we do not have to struggle to attain them, as the Martians would have to do if they had no means of communication with one another at all analogous to human language. But, on pain of circularity, we cannot *use* these concepts in framing our explanation: we cannot take for granted an implicit grasp of these concepts, for they are among the things that have to be made explicit if our explanation is to make perspicuous what we already know without being able to say what it is that we know. We are not in the same position as the imaginary Martians, who were trying to comprehend what we already implicitly comprehend; we are merely trying to render explicit what is implicit. But we shall have succeeded in our task only if the account that we finally construct is one that, if it could be conveyed to them, would satisfy the Martians; and that requires that it should not employ concepts that are intelligible only to those who already have a language comparable to ours.

What about the concept of truth itself, or the concepts of truth and falsity? Is it legitimate to use it, or them, in our philosophical account of language? That depends upon the perspective from which we are viewing our task. Truth is an attribute of what is said, of utterances: so regarded, it is a notion applicable to linguistic items. But it is also an attribute of propositions and of beliefs; it is enough to say 'of propositions' if we take propositions to be the objects of belief—that which is believed. So, if we are viewing our task from the perspective of philosophers of thought, we are entitled to take the concepts of truth and falsity as given in advance of our account of language, since we are supposing ourselves equipped with a prior account of thoughts and of what it is to have them, and the concepts of truth and falsity must already have been explained as applicable to thoughts. But, if we are viewing our task from the perspective of linguistic philosophers, we shall not be crediting ourselves with possessing any prior account of thoughts, and shall therefore not regard ourselves as entitled to avail ourselves of the concepts of truth and falsity without supplying an explanation of them. For in this case our philosophical account of language will be our route to a philosophical account of thought; we shall be seeking to explain a grasp of a concept in terms of a mastery of the uses and meanings of words, and a grasp of a proposition in terms of our understanding of what is meant by the utterance of a sentence.

For the same reason, we must, as linguistic philosophers, eschew appeal to any concept a grasp of which depends upon a grasp of the concepts of truth and falsity. Concepts of this kind include those of believing something to be so and of wishing something to be so. If the significance of someone's uttering the sentence 'There are llamas in that field' assertorically is explained as conveying to the hearer that the speaker intends him to take the speaker as believing that there are llamas in the field, this is an analysis available to the philosopher of thought but not, without a great deal of previous explanation, to the linguistic philosopher. He cannot presume it known what it is to believe that there are llamas in the field until he has first explained what it is to grasp the thought there are llamas in the field and what it is to take that thought to be true; and he is proposing to do this by explaining the meaning of the sentence 'There are llamas in that field', what it is to know what the sentence means and what it is for the sentence to be true. He would go round in a circle if he explained the meaning of an utterance of the sentence in the manner imagined.

To explain how a language functions requires us to specify, for every possible sentence of the language, what difference is potentially made to what subsequently happens by someone's uttering that sentence in any given circumstances. How can we possibly accomplish this? A simple suggestion would be by listing, for each sentence of the language, the significance of uttering it in each of a number of types of context. The utterance of some sentences would have a different significance in different contexts; yet other sentences would be ambiguous, having distinct possible significances in the *same* context. The suggestion is defeated by a decisive objection.

We could not list all sentences that could be formed in a natural language, indeed in anything that deserves to be called a language, because, whatever the language, there will not be a finite number of them: there will be infinitely many possible sentences that can be constructed in the language. In order to frame an exhaustive description covering all those infinitely many possible sentences, we must therefore descend to a level below that of the sentence to the elements from which sentences are formed—words. A language has, at any one time, only a finite vocabulary—otherwise, a comprehensive dictionary would be infinitely long. Words are the semantic atoms. Spoken words are indeed composed of phonemes, and written words of letters; but their meanings are not, in general, determined by their composition: the spoken word 'word' does not share a component of its meaning with 'herd', nor the written word

'word' a component of its meaning with 'lord'. To the extent that there are apparent exceptions to the semantic atomicity of words, we need to recognize a different principle of division into words from that followed by the typographer. You can tell what the word 'unwell' means if you understand the relevant sense of the adjective 'well' and you are familiar with the prefix 'un-'; so that prefix, for semantic purposes, must count as a word, even though it is never written separately. The same goes for the termination '-ed' by which the past tense is formed. Indeed, a semantic unit need not have a uniform phonetic or orthographic form. A child who says 'I bringed it' is making no semantic mistake, but only a syntactic one, not realizing that 'to bring' does not inflect in the same way as 'to bang'; the relevant semantic unit is an abstract one [PAST TENSE]. We have, therefore, to specify the meanings of the words of the language, that is, of its semantic atoms.

This necessity does not arise only from the capacity of the language to generate infinitely many sentences, but from the need to give a realistic account of the understanding of the language that is possessed by its speakers. We understand sentences we hear or read *because* we understand the words of which they are composed, and the principles in accordance with which they are put together. More exactly, it is because we understand sentences in this way that the language is able to generate infinitely many sentences. It remains that we must explain the meaning of any word in terms of its potential occurrence in sentences, that is, as its contribution to determining the significance of any such sentence; for, while words are semantic atoms, sentences remain the primary semantic units, in the sense of the smallest bit of language by means of which it is possible to *say* anything. (In a number of linguistic contexts, notably in answering a question, a sequence of words may be 'understood', in the grammarians' sense, rendering it possible to make a statement, for example, by uttering a single word: in answer to the question 'How many buns are left?', saying 'Two' is tantamount to saying 'There are two buns left'. If the point were pressed, it would become necessary to specify, as the smallest units by which anything could be *said*, words or phrases that, in the given context, are treated as tantamount to sentences. But this is an emendation in response to a quibble.)

An explanation of the meaning of a word must specify the contribution it makes to the significance of a sentence in which it occurs; and, to the extent that it has a single meaning, this contribution must be the same to each of the great variety of such sentences. Many words have a range of related meanings, and the dictionary will enumerate their different senses; but many—the words 'goat' and 'nettle', for example—have only a single meaning, and must make the same contributions to the meanings of all the sentences containing them. But how can we explain this, when the significance of an utterance can be so various? By saying, 'Please introduce me to your brother', I ask someone to do something; by saying 'Either he is your brother or he isn't', I try to induce him to be frank with me; by saying 'I will never speak to my brother again', I declare my intention. Obviously the word 'brother' means the same in all these sentences, and is not used in a transferred sense in any of them, as it is in 'All men are brothers': yet how can there be a uniform contribution to doing all these different things?

Frege took the first step to escaping this dilemma by distinguishing three components of the meaning of a sentence: sense, force, and tone. He used no single word for 'linguistic meaning' in general; but the three features he distinguished are all parts of what must be apprehended if an utterance is to be fully understood. Frege observed, first, that a declarative sentence and the corresponding interrogative form, by which we may ask a question to which the answer will be 'Yes' or 'No', share a common component of their meaning: this he called their *sense*. Both express the obtaining of one and the same possible state of affairs: they differ in that, uttered on its own, the declarative sentence will normally serve to *state* that that state of affairs obtains, while the interrogative one will serve to *ask* whether it obtains. The specification of the state of affairs in question is the *sense* common to both sentences: it is the proposition, or thought in Frege's terminology, that they both express. What differentiates them is the *force* attached to them: to one an assertoric, to the other an interrogative, force. The different force is conventionally indicated by the difference in syntactic form between the two sentences. This is not to say that the declarative sentence always has an assertoric force attached to it; it has such a force only when it functions as a complete sentence. When it is part of a complex sentence—for instance, when it is the antecedent of a conditional—it has *no* force attached to it; for force can be attached only to a complete sentence, not to one that forms part of a longer sentence. Thus, if I say 'If Stephen is Philip's brother, has there been a quarrel between them?', interrogative force is attached to the whole sentence, but neither it nor assertoric force is attached to the subordinate clause: I am neither asking whether nor asserting that Stephen is Philip's brother. Sentences with the conjunctions 'and' and 'but', such as 'Richard has come, but has Jane?', are apparent exceptions; this happens because the utterance of a sentence with these two conjunctions is equivalent to the utterance of the two conjoined clauses as separate sentences.

The remaining ingredient of linguistic meaning, tone, is a ragbag. Frege counted as part of the sense of a sentence only what bears on the truth or falsity of the thought it expresses; everything that determines neither its sense, so characterized, nor the force attached to it, he counted as belonging to its 'tone'. Thus, if someone says 'The Colonel's father is dead', and someone else says 'The Colonel's father is deceased', the difference in their choice of words cannot affect the truth or falsity of what they say; so the difference of meaning is one of tone, not of sense. Again, to use an example of Frege's own, if someone says 'He has not come yet', he is expressing the thought that the man in question has not arrived up to the time of speaking, which could as well be expressed by saying simply 'He has not come'; the word 'yet' serves only to convey, without stating, that the speaker expected him to have come sooner, and probably hopes that he will still arrive, and so it, too, contributes to the tone and not to the sense.

Frege expressly refused to regard imperative or optative sentences as expressing thoughts; but later writers have applied his sense/force distinction to them, treating them as expressing whatever thought or proposition must hold if the imperative is complied with or the wish fulfilled. Thus extended, Frege's tripartite classification of linguistic meaning offers the first hope of our systematizing the contribution made to the meaning of a sentence by its component words. In fact, it offers the only hope that has yet been held out to us; snide criticisms have been made of it, but no one has proposed any other strategy for achieving an account of how the meanings of sentences are determined by their composition. The theory needs some amendment. The ragbag category of tone stands in pressing need of further differentiation; and the notion of force presents us with problems not easy to resolve. Not every difficulty in understanding what someone says is to be resolved by appeal to some established convention. We ask questions like 'What was he driving at?', 'What did that have to do with it?', and 'What was the point of that remark?' These have the general form, 'Why did he say that then?': they go to the *intention* with which the speaker said what he did. The sense of the phrase 'what he said' here usually comprises the force of the utterance: we are asking why the speaker made that assertion or asked that question. Understanding another is frequently a matter of divining his underlying intention; and this is not something for which the language being spoken has provided in advance, or which is peculiar to it, but a non-linguistic question about a linguistic act. Perceiving a speaker's intention is just a special case of perceiving the intention with which someone has performed an action. The difference between this and what

Frege meant by 'force' is clear in principle: in practice, it is often difficult to know how to draw the line between them. This is in part because, in using language as in other matters, we imitate one another: it is difficult to say when a practice frequently repeated has passed into becoming a convention. These are details, however, though important details: in general, there can be no doubt that Frege indicated the strategy that we need to adopt.

4

Truth-Conditional Semantics

It is only against the background of a partition of linguistic meaning into distinguishable components, such as that made by Frege into sense, force, and tone, that what is unquestionably the most popular method for specifying the senses of particular words, expressions, and sentences of the language becomes intelligible. This is to specify them as determining the condition for each sentence (or a particular utterance of it) to be true. It was, again, Frege who devised the first fully articulated version of such a theory of meaning. On his account, to each logically unitary word or expression is associated a semantic value (an expression I am substituting for the somewhat confusing term *Bedeutung* used by Frege). The semantic values of the constituents of a phrase combine to determine a semantic value for the phrase; the semantic values of the constituents of a sentence are designed to combine to determine a value, *true* or *false*, for the sentence. This truth-value is the semantic value of the sentence as a whole. Thus, to take an example of the simplest type, the semantic value of a proper name is an object, and that of a one-place predicate is a function from objects to truth-values; the sentence that results from inserting the proper name in the argument-place of the predicate will have, as its truth-value, the value of the function that is the semantic value of the predicate for that object as argument that is the semantic value of the proper name. For instance, the sentence

'The Earth spins' has the value *true* because the semantic value of the predicate '. . . spins' is a function that maps all spinning objects, including the Earth, onto the value *true*, and all those that do not spin onto the value *false*. (The phrase 'the Earth' is composed of two words, but is a logically unitary proper name like 'Uranus'; no contrast is intended with 'an Earth' or 'another Earth'. Whether or not a language requires the definite article before any given proper name is a mere syntactic convention, like whether it has an initial capital letter.)

The semantic value of an expression is not, on Frege's theory, its sense. The sense of an expression must be capable of being *given* to the mind, whereas what is given can never simply be an object or a function; as Kant said, 'Every object is given to us in a particular way'. The sense of an expression is a particular means of determining its semantic value. But, since nothing irrelevant to the truth or falsity of a sentence in which the expression occurs can be part of its sense, that sense can contain nothing that does not go to determine its semantic value.

This idea was taken up by Wittgenstein in the *Tractatus*, when he wrote, 'To understand a sentence means to know what is the case if it is true', and, in slightly varying forms, it has remained with us ever since as the 'truth-conditional theory of meaning'. Whether a particular sentence is true depends, of course, not only on its sense, but on how things are in the world; but, according to this conception, to understand the sentence is to know how things must be in the world for it to be true. Various arguments, to my mind unconvincing, have been put forward to deny any need, in specifying the meanings of the words of a language, for a separate or explicit characterization of force or of tone; but it is agreed, on all but a few hands, that the *central* ingredient of meaning, that which Frege called 'sense', is to be explained in terms of an expression's contribution to determining the condition for the truth of any sentence that contains it.

Frege was a strong adherent of the principle of bivalence, which states that every sentence that has a definite sense, considered, when necessary, as uttered on a particular occasion by a particular speaker, is determinately either true or false. He did not believe that existing natural languages conformed to the principle: quite the contrary. Two features of natural languages cause them to violate bivalence: the possibility of forming singular terms such as definite descriptions like 'the centre of the universe', which have a sense but fail to denote any object, and the existence of proper names of which the same holds good; and the existence of predicates that are not well defined, or not defined at all, for every object. A sentence such as 'There were many mountains on Atlantis' or 'There were many mountains on the lost continent' fails to be either true or false because there is no object denoted by the name 'Atlantis' or by the definite description 'the lost continent'; one such as 'Munich is populous' fails to be determinately either true or false because the predicate '. . . is populous' is not well (that is, sharply) defined, while such a sentence as 'Munich is cowardly' is neither true nor false because the predicate '. . . is cowardly' is not defined at all for cities. Rather, the principle of bivalence was for Frege a requirement for a language that could operate with perfect reliability as an instrument for deductive reasoning. To obtain such an instrument, either an artificial language must be created or a natural language refashioned so as to satisfy the principle of bivalence.

In fashioning an artificial language for this purpose, or refashioning a natural one, every predicate must be so explained that it is determinate, for every object, whether it applies to it or not. This requirement is repeatedly stated by Frege; but, each time that he states it, he hastens to add that it is not necessary that *we* should be able to decide, for any object, whether or not the predicate holds good of it: all that is demanded is that it should be impersonally determined whether or not it does. We might put it in this way: *we* do not need to be able to tell whether the predicate is true or false of the object: but *reality* must determine either that it is true of it or that it is false of it. We indeed confer upon the predicate whatever sense it has, thus determining the condition that any object must satisfy if the predicate is to be true of that object; in grasping the sense of the predicate, we *know what it is* for it to apply to an object, but we do not need to have a means of recognizing whether or not the object satisfies the condition for it to do so. What goes for predicates must go for all linguistic expressions, including sentences. We have assigned to the sentences of our language the senses that they bear, and, if they are to conform to the principle of bivalence, these must be such as to render them either true or false. Their senses determine the conditions under which they are true, and, in grasping those senses, we apprehend those truth-conditions; but it need not be within our capacity to tell whether those conditions obtain. *Reality* determines whether the sentence is true or false; it is irrelevant whether we can do so or not, so long as we know *what it is for* the sentence to be true.

This Fregean or truth-conditional account of sense makes a grasp of sense unequivocally into the possession of a piece of theoretical *knowledge*. We have seen that it is a requirement upon any acceptable theory of meaning that it be capable of supporting a viable account of understanding; and the concept of understanding is unquestionably closely allied to that of knowledge. We use the phrase 'to know what [a given expression] means' interchangeably with 'to understand [that expression]'; and, in the observation previously quoted from the *Tractatus*, 'To understand a sentence means to know what is the case if it is true', Wittgenstein equated understanding a sentence with *knowing* the condition for it to be true. Now knowledge has traditionally been categorized as either theoretical or practical: as knowing *that* something is so or as knowing *how* to do something. The classification is inadequate. We all know what it is for someone to execute a high jump; what only few of us know is how to do it. But when you learn to dance the rumba, you are not merely acquiring the practical ability to do something of which you already knew precisely what it is to do it. Before you learned, you had only a vague idea of what it was to do it; you could be deceived by someone making with assurance movements that looked to you like those made by people of whom you were told that they were dancing the rumba. In learning to dance the rumba, you are not merely learning *how* to do it, but learning *what it is* to do it; the knowledge that you acquire lies midway between theoretical and practical knowledge. You may be said to have learned *that* dancing the rumba requires certain movements, and this differentiates the knowledge that you have acquired from merely knowing how to do something; but that knowledge need not be able to be expressed in words, which differentiates it from theoretical or propositional knowledge. It is only if you are unable to express it in words, or at least unable to do so without a considerable effort of thought, that it is, in the form in which you have it, knowledge of a kind intermediate between the standard types of theoretical and practical knowledge. Asked what the rumba is, you can only *demonstrate* it: you say, 'The steps are like this', and show what the steps are. You have come to know something that you did not know before; but not anything that you can *state*.

Learning a language is acquiring knowledge of this intermediate variety. The absurdity of the answer 'I don't know, I've never tried' to the question 'Can you speak Portuguese?' arises from the fact that, in order to speak Portuguese, you have to *know* something, indeed a good deal. But the knowledge in question is of the intermediate kind. Until you know Portuguese, you do not really know what it is to speak Portuguese, and could be deceived by someone uttering nonsense words. If Portuguese is a second language for you, much of your knowledge of it may be explicit theoretical knowledge, especially if you have learned it out of a book; but, if it were your mother tongue, very little of your knowledge of it would be likely to be of this type.

There is an active and a passive knowledge of a language: the ability to speak it and write in it, and the ability to hear, read, and understand it. Someone who had only the passive, not the active, ability might be said to know the language without being able to speak it; the dialogue about Portuguese would not in his case be comic. If it frequently happened that people found themselves with an inexplicable inhibition against speaking certain languages, someone might know a number of languages, although able to speak only a few of them. But to represent anyone's knowledge of his mother tongue as being theoretical knowledge, rather than knowledge of the intermediate kind, is to be guilty of offering a circular explanation.

At least, the explanation is circular if offered by a linguistic philosopher. For the linguistic philosopher, the theory of meaning, and the theory of understanding that is built upon it, form the only route to a philosophical account of thought; only by explaining what it is to understand the sentences of a language can we explain what it is to grasp the propositions we express by means of language. But, if we attempt to explain the understanding of a sentence as consisting in the possession of a piece of knowledge about that sentence, our explanation is circular: we are trying to explain grasping one proposition—that expressed by the sentence—in terms of judging another—the proposition that the sentence is true under such-and-such conditions—to be true. If we follow the linguistic philosopher's strategy of explanation, we cannot avail ourselves of the notion of theoretical knowledge until we have constructed our theory of meaning and the theory of understanding that rests upon it, or at least have sketched the plan of their construction.

These strictures do not apply to the philosopher of thought. He is wholly entitled to assume a grasp of propositions, and a knowledge of their truth, antecedent to a knowledge of language, and to explain the latter in terms of the former: that is his whole strategy. But, if he attempts to give a truth-conditional account of the content of a proposition or a thought, exactly parallel strictures will then apply to it: the circularity will be even more flagrant. Such a truth-conditional account of content will take the form of the truth-conditional account of meaning with all reference to linguistic items deleted. The senses of expressions will be replaced by thought-constituents. Such thought-constituents will be related to their external correlates as, on Frege's theory, the senses of expressions were related to the semantic values of those expressions: they will be particular ways of determining those external correlates—objects, properties, and relations. The external correlates of the constituents of a thought or proposition will together determine the truth-value of that proposition. And a grasp of the proposition will consist in a knowledge of how things must be for the proposition to have the value *true*. Such an account of the matter will indeed be flagrantly circular: the grasp of an arbitrary proposition will be being explained by the knowledge of the condition for the truth of that proposition.

Neither as a theory of meaning nor as an autonomous theory of content can an account in terms of truth-conditions escape a fatal circularity.

Truth-conditional theories of meaning and of content are irredeemably circular. It might be objected that they have a more serious defect: they use the notion of truth without explaining it. But this objection would be unfair. We do not need to think of a truth-conditional account of sense as a bare specification of truth-conditions, standing on its own; it is better thought of as located within a comprehensive theory of meaning, comprising force and tone as well as sense. Presumably the truth-conditional account of content is similarly located within a comprehensive theory of thought, comprising propositional attitudes such as judgement and belief as well as the mere grasp of propositions. The assignments of senses to words (semantic atoms) of the language, and the consequent assignments of truth-conditions to sentences of the language, though it may occupy the major part of a fully comprehensive theory of meaning, should be seen as no more than a *preparation* for what follows. What is to follow is an account of the *use* of the language, that is, of the significance of any utterance in it. In giving such an account, we should have to *use* the notion of truth as it applies to any given sentence; it is from the use thus made of it that the notion of truth gains its content.

A statement of the rules of a card game may begin with a specification, which may be simple and may be complicated, of the order in which the cards rank: some may be trumps, and they will rank in a particular order, while the cards of the plain suits may rank in a different order. All this, however, is only a preliminary to the rules of play that follow. It is significant only in so far as the ranking of the cards figures in those rules—for example, in determining who has won a given trick. When you know only the order in which the cards rank, you as yet know nothing about how to play the game. Similarly, when you know only the truth-conditions of the sentences of a language, you as yet know nothing about how to speak the language.

This remark might seem absurd: have not Davidson and others proposed that a specification of the truth-conditions of the sentences of a language may be viewed as constituting a complete theory of meaning for that language? When I know the condition under which a declarative sentence of the language is true, do I not know what a speaker who utters it is saying, and thereby the significance of his utterance? You know that only if you implicitly understand the connection between the condition for the truth of a sentence and its use, and hence know something that the theory has failed to make explicit: a theory of truth for a language can masquerade as a theory of meaning only by trading on a substantial piece of implicit knowledge on the part of those who study it. This becomes evident if we imagine the theory stated by using, for the semantic values of sentences, not the familiar words 'true' and 'false', but some pair of hitherto unknown words. We should certainly then be under no impression that we had been provided with an adequate theory of meaning for the language. Even if we guessed that the two words denoted the two truth-values, we should not know which stood for the value *true* and which for the value *false* until we knew how the sentences were in practice *used*. It is what would have to be explained, concerning the newly introduced pair of terms, which we implicitly know concerning the terms 'true' and 'false', and which ought to be made explicit by any fully explanatory theory of meaning.

It is the task of a comprehensive theory of meaning to make explicit everything that must be implicitly grasped by a fully competent speaker of the language, and hence everything that has to be learned by an infant before he can become such a speaker; for only by doing so can the theory shed a philosophical light that illuminates the whole space occupied by those concepts that puzzle us when we contemplate language. These concepts, enormously familiar to us in our everyday lives, profoundly obscure when we attempt to elucidate them philosophically, are those of language itself, of meaning, of a proposition, of content, of assertion, and of truth and falsity; and it becomes of especial importance to elucidate the latter pair when it is proposed to explain the sense of an arbitrary sentence by appeal to what determines it as true or as false.

It is the theory of force that primarily serves to explain the significance of linguistic utterances. An utterance by means of which the speaker makes a request of the hearer gains its significance from two things: the fact that it *is* a request; and the particular thing requested. Use of the distinction between sense and force liberates us from having to explain these two features separately for each such sentence piecemeal; that is the whole point of the distinction. Rather, we shall regard the sentence as embodying the expression of a proposition to which is attached the force that characterizes the utterance as a request. The proposition in question will be that which will be rendered true if the request is granted. The theory of force will give a description of the social practice of making requests, granting and refusing them; it will thus provide a uniform explanation of the linguistic expression of a request, whatever the particular content of the request. The proposition to which the requesting force is attached will, like all propositions, be capable of being true or of being false. We do not normally say of a request that it is true or that it is false, but that it is granted or refused, just as we do not normally say of a question to be answered 'Yes' or 'No' that it is true or that it is false, but only that the correct answer was one or the other. An account of the functioning of a language that appeals to the distinction between sense and force requires us to regard the specific contents of a wide variety of non-assertoric utterances as constituted by propositions to which some non-assertoric force has been attached; and there is of course no impropriety in calling any such proposition 'true' or 'false'.

It is to assertions that those epithets are most naturally applied. Assertoric force is far more complex to explain than interrogative force or the force that renders an utterance a request. A question is a request for information or for explanation; once we know how information is communicated or an explanation given, there is no difficulty in characterizing interrogative force. It is by means of assertions that we communicate information; and so an adequate account of assertoric force must explain the difficult concept of information. What presently concerns us, however, is that it is from the practice of making assertions that our notions of truth and falsity originally derive. It is a central feature of assertions that they can be right or wrong; any account of the assertoric use of language must incorporate this feature. Moreover, in a great many cases, it is possible for an assertion to be *proved* to have been right or to have been wrong. Our primitive notion of truth and falsity equates the truth of a sentence, as uttered by a particular speaker on a particular occasion, with the correctness of an assertion made by uttering it, and its falsity with the incorrectness of such an assertion.

Almost everyone who has written about the topic has stated that the anti-realist raises two objections to a truth-conditional account of sense or content, and, more especially, of understanding. First, that the knowledge in which the understanding of a sentence or of an expression is alleged by the account to consist cannot, in general, be fully manifested; and, secondly, that there is no explaining how this knowledge could be acquired. Both these are serious charges. Possession of a piece of knowledge must make a difference to the possessor: it is unintelligible to attribute to an agent knowledge that can never in any way affect what he does or even what he says. Equally, to have a piece of knowledge, there must have been a way of coming by it, at least unless it may plausibly be claimed to be something that everyone knows as soon as he is able to grasp its content, which is certainly not the case for a speaker's knowledge of his mother tongue. There are many other things it must be possible to say about a piece of knowledge if anyone can truly be credited with possessing it. In particular, if a piece of knowledge is to be used, it must be delivered when needed; it must therefore be possible to say in what form it is delivered to the agent. But neither the objection arising from the manifestation nor that arising from the acquisition of the knowledge is central. The central objection is the circularity of a truth-conditional account.

Most defendants of the truth-conditional theory simply ignore this circularity. Truly honest ones, such as Gareth Evans, a pioneer in the philosophy of thought who adhered to a truth-conditional account of content, admit their inability to explain a grasp of meaning or content without circularity. 'The difficulty', Evans wrote in his brilliant posthumous book *The Varieties of Reference*, 'is to give any substance to the notion of knowing what it is for a proposition to be true . . . I am quite unable to give a general account of this notion' (p. 106). He was nevertheless convinced that it was the right notion to use, and that it was possible to give some credible account of it, and used it, and the corresponding notion of knowing what it is for a given predicate to be true of an arbitrary object, throughout the rest of the book.

Few proponents of truth-conditional theories of meaning acknowledge that there is anything they have failed to explain. Gareth Evans's adherence to the truth-conditional conception was an act of faith. Such faith stands in need of a rational foundation.

5

Justificationist Theories of Meaning

What forces a truth-conditional theory of meaning or of content to be circular? And what would a non-circular theory be like? A non-circular theory of meaning would represent a knowledge of the meaning of a sentence or word as knowing how to use that sentence or word; a non-circular theory of content would represent a grasp of a proposition or of one of its constituent concepts as knowing how to frame that proposition or some range of propositions involving that concept and to act on it or them. This knowledge would not consist merely in a practical ability, however complex. It would comprise an extensive knowledge of facts; at least this would be so when linguistic knowledge was in question. But the knowledge would be of the intermediate type: the facts known would not be statable in words, or at least not so statable by the subject. For this reason, there would be no circularity in the account.

As we saw, Frege felt unable to give a non-circular explanation of this kind. If he had felt able to do so, he might have identified a grasp of the sense of a predicate with an ability to decide, for any object, whether the predicate was true of it or not. Such an ability need not be displayed by any propensity to make specific gestures of assent or dissent, such as those imagined by Quine, in response to utterances applying the predicate to various objects; it is enough for it to be displayed by a willingness or unwillingness to make or to accept such predications. A description of the linguistic practice of making assertions must include the possible reactions of the hearer. These will depend on whether or not the hearer accepts the assertion; and so an account of assertoric force must incorporate the notion of someone's accepting what was said to him as true. There need be no uniform token of such acceptance—the linguistic behaviour of adult human beings is more complicated than that. But the notion of a speaker's accepting a statement will of necessity figure in any account of the practice of speaking the language; and he must in some manner, however complex, be capable of manifesting which statements he accepts—'holds-true', in Davidson's terminology—and which he rejects. On a non-circular account of understanding, the grasp of the sense of a predicate could be taken to consist in an ability to arrive at a correct decision, for any given object, whether to accept or reject a statement applying that predicate to that object.

Why did Frege feel himself unable to give such a non-circular explanation? For the obvious reason that, for many predicates, there is no effective method for deciding, for any arbitrary object, whether a given such predicate is true of it or not. The obstacles to arriving at such a decision are not merely practical: there is often no method of deciding even in principle—which means supposing all practical obstacles overcome. And so Frege had to fall back on saying, not that we can determine whether the predicate applies, but, impersonally, that it *is determined* whether or not it applies. Our grasp of its sense will therefore consist, not in an ability to determine whether or not it is true of any given object, but in the *knowledge* of what will determine whether or not it is true of it; the knowledge of what it is for the predicate to be true of an object. This knowledge cannot be explained as knowledge, even of the intermediate kind, of how to do anything: it is irredeemably propositional knowledge—theoretical knowledge which, if we have it at all, we can have only by being able to express it. It is from that that the circularity arises.

When we do have an effective means of determining the application of a predicate, as we do for the simple observational predicates such as '... is soft', '... is smooth', '... is green', and the like that are the first that we learn, knowing what it is for it to be true of an object may be equated with being able to *tell* whether it is true of that object. There are many predicates whose application we have no effective means of determining, however. This is a simple consequence of the fact that there are propositions that we can express but whose truth-value we have no effective means of determining; for, as Frege held, a one-place predicate is, in general, simply what is left of a sentence when we have removed from it one or more occurrences of some proper name or other singular term. A theory of meaning according to which we have attached a genuine sense only to those sentences the truth-value of utterances of which we have an effective method of deciding ought to be rejected out of hand; for our language allows us to frame a great many sentences that we understand perfectly well but for which we have no such effective method. These may be termed 'undecidable sentences', as long as it is borne in mind that 'undecidable', in this use, means 'not effectively decidable'; sentences whose truth-value we do have an effective method of deciding may be termed 'decidable'. But need a non-circular account of sense assume so crude a form as to deny all sense to undecidable sentences?

Although we may have no means, even in principle, of putting ourselves into a position in which we can effectively decide whether the proposition expressed by the utterance of a given sentence is or is not true, it does not follow that we may not come to *recognize* that proposition as true or as false; we may sometimes, and indeed often do, decide the truth or falsity of utterances of undecidable sentences, in the sense I gave to this expression. A simple type of example is a universally quantified sentence, which we can judge to be false as soon as a counter-instance presents itself, but which, until one occurs, we have no certain means of judging true or false. Of a sentence such that we could in no circumstances correctly judge, in accordance with its sense, that an utterance of it was true or was false, it would indeed be dubious in the extreme that we had conferred on it a sense at all. This suggests a far more plausible variety of non-circular explanation of understanding. According to an explanation of this type, the understanding of a sentence (as uttered on a given occasion) is to be taken to consist in an ability, when suitably placed, to recognize whether it is true or false, even though no effective method exists for so placing oneself. It is no objection to a theory of this type that we so understand certain statements that we should recognize nothing as *conclusively* establishing them as true or as false. A grasp of the sense of a statement of this kind will consist, on such a theory, of an ability to recognize evidence for it when presented with it, and to judge correctly whether or not it is outweighed by any given piece of counter-evidence. We need a label for this type of non-circular alternative to a truth-conditional theory of meaning. The term 'verificationist' has misleading associations; let us call it a 'justificationist' theory.

In the phrase 'an ability, when suitably placed, to recognize the truth or falsity of the proposition', the expression 'when suitably placed' must be understood in accordance with our *actual* methods of judging the truth of what is said. These do not reduce to mere sensory observation. Even for decidable sentences, our means of determining their truth-value may involve mental operations such as counting or physical ones such as measuring. Our sentences cannot be divided into two classes, empirical and a priori, the truth of the one to be decided by raw observation and the truth of the other by unalloyed ratiocination. Rather, they lie on a scale, at one end of which stand the purely observational sentences and at the other mathematical ones arrived at by unaided deduction. Most sentences occupy some position in between: their truth is to be established by a mixture of observation and of reasoning, deductive or otherwise. To have the capacity to recognize a statement as true or as false 'when suitably placed' means to be able so to recognize it when informed of the relevant observations and presented with the relevant reasoning.

Why, then, did Frege not propose this more moderate type of non-circular explanation? What blocked him from adopting a justificationist theory was his unshakable commitment to the principle of bivalence, as one holding good of the thoughts to be expressed in a scientific language—namely, one in which deductive reasoning could be carried out with total confidence; the principle, that is, that any statement with a definite sense must be determinately either true or false. If a sentence in such a language is undecidable, not only do we lack an effective method of deciding whether a given utterance of it is true or false: we have no right to assume that there is anything that, if we were to hit on it, would show us that it was true or that it was false. But, if it is subject to the principle of bivalence, it must *be* either true or false; and it must be in virtue of the sense that we have conferred upon that sentence that reality determines it as the one or as the other. It therefore could not be that a full grasp of that sense would consist solely in an ability to recognize it as having one or other truth-value in those special circumstances in which we were in a position to do so. If it did, then the sense of the sentence would not provide for what would make it true, and what would make it false, in other circumstances. On the assumption of bivalence, a complete grasp of the sense of the sentence would therefore amount to knowing how its truth-value is determined by reality, regardless of whether we are ever in a position to tell what that truth-value is; that is, to knowing how things must stand in reality for it to be true.

A justificationist theory of meaning tallies very well with our actual experience of acquiring language. What we learn is precisely in which circumstances we are entitled, in our own right, as it were, to make this or that assertion. We are, of course, entitled to assert something on the strength of someone else's having asserted it, provided that there is no reason to suppose that person to have been misled or insincere; the phrase 'in our own right' was intended to set such a case aside, and single out those in which the speaker is the, or an, original source of the information. We learn, thus, how, when suitably placed, to recognize as true or as false the statements whose senses we come to know. We also learn, for decidable statements, by what means we can so place ourselves as to decide their truth or falsity. But by what means could we possibly come to know in what a statement's *being* true consists, when we have no means of telling that it is true? What would constitute our having such a piece of knowledge?

Our capacity to recognize statements as true, and hence to know when we are entitled to assert them, does not, indeed, exhaust our progressive mastery of our language. We are not mere instruments for registering states of affairs that we can observe or infer to obtain. If a dog were trained to give various different signals in particular observable circumstances, such as the post's arriving, the front door's remaining open when nobody is there, and so on, we might say 'He's telling us that the post has arrived', but could not rightly say 'He's *saying that* the post has arrived'. The aspect would be entirely altered if he proved capable of spontaneously and intelligently reacting to another dog's giving any of these signals. And that, of course, is what we learn to do when we learn language: to accept the assertions of others as true, and to act on their truth. A child can be said to be saying that something is so only if he has not only learned to tell, by his own capacities, when it is so, but will, when occasion presents itself, act on its being so when he has been told by others that it is. Only if he does this has he entered into the communal practice of using language. No reason presents itself, however, for supposing that, in order to accept what he is told and act on it, he need know anything more about the statements he has learned to understand than when and by what means one can tell that they are true or that they are false, and what is an appropriate response to their truth. He will know what is an appropriate response when he has come to incorporate whatever he has accepted as true into his picture of the world.

The truth-conditional theory, on the other hand, *cannot* give the correct account of the matter: popular with philosophers it may be, and dignified by its endorsement by Frege and the early Wittgenstein; but its circularity condemns it as failing to explain what it was intended to explain. An account of linguistic practice requires the concept of recognizing-as-true, that of accepting-as-true, and that of acting-on-the-truth-of; it is unclear that it needs the concept of *being-true*.

A justificationist theory of meaning thus cannot sustain the principle of bivalence. For bivalence implies that there may be true statements whose truth we, however well placed, are unable, even in principle, to recognize. Since our understanding of such a statement must involve a knowledge of what would constitute it as true, acceptance of the principle demands the adoption of a truth-conditional conception of meaning and the rejection of a justificationist one. The justificationist conception therefore also prompts a rejection of the law of excluded middle. The law of excluded middle is the reflection, within logic, of the semantic principle of bivalence; it states that, for any statement **A**, the statement "**A or not A**" is true. Under some semantic theories in which the principle of bivalence fails, the law of excluded middle remains valid. Given that a statement is to be reckoned false when and only when its negation is true, this can be so only when it is possible for a disjunctive statement "**A or B**" to be true even though neither **A** nor **B** is true. For instance, a semantics for vague statements might treat a statement as true only when it definitely held good; and then a statement of the form 'That is either red or orange', said of something on the borderline between the two colours, might rank as true, although neither 'That is red' nor 'That is orange' was true.

Now, under a justificationist conception of meaning, we might well be regarded as entitled to assert a statement "**A or B**" when we have an effective means of putting ourselves in a position to recognize either **A** or **B** as true; for instance, when **A** is a decidable statement and **B** is "**Not A**" (we then have an instance of the law of excluded middle). This, however, is not a genuine parallel to the 'red'/'orange' example. There is no need for a justificationist to restrict justifiability to statements whose truth we have established; he may regard a statement as justifiable whenever we have an effective means in principle of coming to recognize its truth. We are not entitled to make assertions unless their truth has been established, or at least found to have evidence in their favour; but a statement we are not at present entitled to assert may nevertheless be justifiable if we possess the means to establish its truth, even if we do not as yet know that we do. Under this more lenient characterization of justifiability, if **A** is decidable, then either it or its negation is justifiable; the disjunction "**A or not A**", which we shall be entitled to assert, will then not be one neither of whose constituent sentences is justifiable.

From this it is apparent that we may be entitled to assert some instances of the law of excluded middle "**A or not A**" when we are not yet entitled to assert either **A** or "**Not A**"; but we cannot assert all instances of it. Much turns on how the connective '**or**' is to be interpreted in a justificationist semantics. If it is understood in such a way that "**A or B**" can be asserted only when we have the means of establishing either **A** or **B** as true, it will follow immediately that "**A or not A**" can never be asserted if **A** is an undecidable and as yet undecided statement. Without much closer enquiry, we are not able to say that there cannot be undecidable statements **A** and **B** such that we could establish the truth of "**A or B**" without being in a position to establish that of **A** or of **B**. This *would* be a genuine parallel to the 'red'/'orange' example. But this possibility does not give us a general licence to assert "**A or not A**" for undecidable **A**. It might be objected that we are *always* entitled to assert that: it may be regarded as having been 'established' in all circumstances without further enquiry. Such an objection, however, is prompted only by adherence, not as yet dispelled, to the principle of bivalence: the conviction that either **A** or "**Not A**" must be true. A justificationist conception of meaning denies that we are in possession—*could be* in possession—of a notion of truth that will sustain this conviction. It follows that, if we adopt a justificationist theory of meaning, as, I have argued, we are compelled to do, we must reject the law of excluded middle as a universally valid logical law. With it, we must therefore also reject classical logic, normally taken as resting on the two-valued semantics that embodies the principle of bivalence. We have, rather, to admit only those modes of deductive reasoning recognized as valid under intuitionistic logic. What a deductive argument, to be valid, must preserve from premises to conclusion is *justifiability*, where a statement is justifiable if it is possible to justify it.

Must we, then, jettison the concept of truth in favour of that of justifiability? If we were to do this, our semantic theory would be deprived of all metaphysical resonance; for, as we saw, it is by the correspondence between facts and true propositions that a semantic theory acquires such resonance. If our semantic theory loses that resonance, it will fail to attribute to the speakers of the language any conception of the reality about which they speak. Such a conception is, however, an integral part of everyone's understanding of language; for metaphysics is not the specialized interest of metaphysicians, but, in however confused or inchoate a form, part of everybody's mental equipment. More generally, we gradually build up in our minds a picture of the world we inhabit; and this picture guides our actions. Precisely that is what happens when we accept as true a statement that is made to us: we add to or modify our picture of the world, which forms the basis of our subsequent actions. We therefore cannot simply jettison the concept of truth; rather, we must adapt our notion of truth in the light of our conception of what constitutes an understanding of language.

We ought not, therefore, to repudiate the formula 'To understand a sentence is to know what it is for it to be true'; rather, we must enquire with what conception of truth we must replace that held (but never clearly explained) by the truth-conditional theorist. The truth-conditional theorist's conception of truth is a strongly *realist* one. Realism is the belief in a reality independent of our knowledge of it and of our means of attaining such knowledge, which renders our statements true when they are true and false when they are false. When realism is characterized in this highly general way, it behoves us all to be realists to a large degree. Every infant learns, gradually but rather rapidly, that he is living within an objectively existing world that is to a great extent independent of his will—and even independent of his beliefs about it—which is not wholly but is in the main stable within his time span, and which contains others beside himself. It is not up to any philosopher to challenge this fundamental acknowledgement of the objectivity and independence of reality. The characterization of some philosophical view concerning a particular topic as realistic has substance only by contrast with an opposing view that has been maintained or is at least imaginable. We may say that a philosopher is guilty of *extravagant realism* when he postulates facts of a spurious kind, in which there is no good reason to believe, as rendering our statements true or false. I have been maintaining that the realism implicit in a truth-conditional semantics is extravagant.

What conception of truth ought we to adopt in the light of a justificationist theory of meaning? Since truth and meaning must be explained together, it lies to hand to identify the truth of a statement with its justifiability. This answer requires a detailed gloss, since to say that a statement *can* be justified demands an elucidation of the sense in which 'can' is being used. Suppose, first, that **A** is a decidable statement that has not yet in fact been recognized as true. Then, as we have seen, the particular instance "**A or not A**" of the law of excluded middle will be justifiable, and, furthermore, assertable. For, by applying the procedure for deciding whether **A** holds or not, we shall establish the truth either of **A** or of its negation; it follows that the disjunction of them *can* be justified.

How does this bear on the truth or falsity of **A** itself? There are two ways in which we may look at the matter. One would be to say that, since neither **A** nor its negation has been established, and may never be, neither of them is true: in respect of the question 'Does **A** hold or not?', reality is indeterminate. Since we have agreed to accept "**A or not A**" as true, we should, if we adopted this view, really be in the position of allowing that a disjunctive statement can be true even though neither of its component subsentences is true.

This may well be thought to involve too radical an affront to our realist dispositions. If we cleave to the conventional idea that a disjunctive statement can be true only if one or both of its subsentences is true, we shall be compelled to adopt the common-sense view that **A** is either true or false, although we do not know, and may never know, which. On this account, either **A** or its negation is true, because either the one or the other *could* be verified. We have a procedure for deciding whether or not **A** is true. If we were to apply it, we should come up with a verification either of **A** or of its negation. So either **A** or "**Not A**" must be true, though, until we apply the procedure, we do not know which. Thus, if the result of carrying out the decision procedure were that the statement proved to be true, we should in fact have an effective means of establishing its truth, even though we did not know that we had one, and correspondingly for its negation; and so either the statement or its negation will qualify as being true even though we have not carried out the procedure, and may never do so.

This reasoning, as stated, embodies a logical fallacy. We cannot validly infer from a subjunctive conditional of the form "**If it were the case that B, then it would be the case that either C or D**" the disjunction of the subjunctive conditionals "**If it were the case that B, then it would be the case that C**" and "**If it were the case that B, then it would be the case that D**". Thus it may be that, if I had given certain information to Jean, she would have passed it on to either Clare or Helen; it cannot be inferred that it is either true that, given the information, Jean would have passed it on to Clare, or true that, given the information, she would have passed it on to Helen: which would have happened might depend on whether Jean had chanced to meet Clare or Helen first, or on a number of other relevant circumstances.

An empirically decidable statement differs from a mathematically decidable one. Of a given natural number, we may legitimately assert that it is either prime or composite without yet knowing which, on the strength of our having an effective procedure for deciding which it is. Moreover, before we apply the procedure, we are entitled to assume that the number *is* determinately either prime or composite. This is because the outcome of the procedure depends only upon our carrying it out correctly, and it is determined in advance what constitutes carrying it out correctly. But the outcome of an empirical decision procedure does not depend only upon our carrying it out correctly: it depends also upon what we are presented with at various steps when we carry it out. Whether or not an empirically decidable statement has a determinate truth-value in advance of our discovering it is not subject to a general ruling applicable to all such statements. It depends on whether, in the particular case, we have reason to suppose it to be determinate what the outcome of the decision procedure would be at each stage.

An example is this. We can, by counting them, determine whether the number of apples in a basket is prime or composite. If we do count them, we may find, say, that it was prime. Should we suppose that it *became* prime only upon our discovering that it was? Or should we assume that it was already prime before we carried out the test? Or, again, can we take it that the number was determinate as long as we were able to determine it, but becomes indeterminate once the apples, not having been counted, are dispersed and so no longer capable of being counted? If we allow that the number was either prime or composite when we were able to count the apples, do we have good grounds for holding it still to be either prime or composite now that the opportunity to find out which it was has been irrevocably lost?

We cannot hold that the proposition that the number of apples is prime was indeterminate in truth-value before the apples were counted because a proposition of this kind rests upon more specific and more fundamental propositions; if its truth-value is indeterminate, then so are those of the more fundamental propositions. The indeterminacy of the proposition that the number of apples is prime would entail the indeterminacy either of the proposition 'No apple was removed or went out of existence at the moment of counting' or of at least one proposition of the form 'That apple was already there before they were counted'. The truth of these propositions is, however, a presupposition of our using the number of apples when counted as yielding the number of those present before they were counted; so we may assume that the apples have been under sufficiently close observation over the relevant period to secure their truth. But in this case the possibility of their being indeterminate in truth-value does not arise; and so the proposition that the number of apples was prime cannot have been indeterminate before they were counted.

How, then, does the case stand when the decision procedure is not carried out? Can we suppose that the proposition had a determinate truth-value while it was still possible to discover it, but ceased to possess one as soon as the opportunity passed? Or that the proposition never had a determinate truth-value? The argument against either of these claims is similar. For it to be indeterminate whether the number of apples was prime or composite, say at the last moment when it was possible to count them, it has to be indeterminate which particular apples were then in the basket; but this supposition is senseless. To identify an individual apple at some given moment requires observation of its location; it therefore cannot be indeterminate whether any one of the apples in the basket was in the basket.

Here, then, we have a case in which we have grounds for holding there to be a fact of the matter what the outcome of the decision procedure would be before it was carried out, or would have been had it been carried out. We therefore have a decidable statement for which not only is the law of excluded middle valid, but for which bivalence holds. Its crucial feature was its resting upon more fundamental propositions known not to be indeterminate. In an example lacking this feature, matters will stand differently. The statement 'The flower under the oak-tree is blue' is decidable; if no one goes to inspect the flower, it will not be decided. Certainly we are entitled to assert 'Either it is blue or it is not', in virtue of the possibility of deciding the question; but no compelling reason appears for holding that its colour must be determinate even if we never inspect the flower, or in advance of our inspecting it. There are no more fundamental propositions whose truth-value cannot be indeterminate, but would be if the colour of the flower were indeterminate: nothing, therefore, to guarantee that the proposition about its colour is either true or false if we never find out which, or even before we find that out.

When we first learn language, it is to the use of decidable predicates and decidable statements that we are first introduced. It could not be otherwise: how could a child *first* be trained to use undecidable ones? How, then, do undecidable statements ever come to be framed? This happens because we learn to use operators which, when applied to decidable sentences, convert them into undecidable ones. Among such operators are quantifiers ranging over infinite or possibly infinite totalities, particularly those such as 'will always', 'will at some time', 'will never', which range over all future time. We first learn to understand quantification over small surveyable totalities such as the plates in a cupboard; we learn that the truth or falsity of a statement about all or some of the plates in a cupboard may be established by inspecting them, and also what to expect when such a statement is made to us.

We carry these expectations over when we progress to quantification over finite but unsurveyable totalities. Statements involving such quantification are decidable in principle, though not in practice. Our understanding of such statements rests in part on our knowledge of when we can in practice verify or falsify them, in part on our forming the right expectations when they are made to us, in part on our knowing by what means they could in principle be decided, and in part on our learning to base justifiable but defeasible generalizations on sufficiently large samples.

The transition to quantification over infinite totalities is very smooth: we carry over everything except the conception of a decision procedure possible in principle. But it is just the lack of this conception that prevents us from having a notion of truth for these statements according to which each is determinately either true or false. From where could we gain a conception of what it is for such a statement to *be* true, even though we have no means of establishing its truth? So far as I can see, only by extending our notion of a means of deciding its truth-value. *We* cannot inspect each member of an infinite totality as we can inspect each of the plates in a cupboard; but perhaps a being with greater powers than ours could do so. We can imagine such a being, and on the idea of his determining the truth of a statement about all its members base our grasp of the statement's being true despite our inability to tell for certain that it is.

This is the defence of, or route to, realism that Gareth Evans called 'ideal verificationism': the idea that we can base our understanding of some range of sentences, and our grasp of what it is for them to be true, on the procedure for deciding their truth or falsity that would be available to an imagined being with superhuman powers, though it lies far beyond what we are able to do. Evans rejected this defence or route; I confess that I have not been able to understand what alternative he proposed. Certainly in the present case ideal verificationism is misconceived. The reason why we cannot survey an infinite totality is not the deficiency of human capabilities: it is that it is *senseless* to imagine an infinite task completed. An infinite task is by definition one that cannot in principle be completed.[1] Our understanding of statements involving quantification over an infinite totality cannot consist in any fiction about their being decided by superhuman observers, nor in any conception of what it is for them to be true, but only in our grasp of how they may be justified in particular cases and of what to expect if we accept them.

What notion of truth ought we, then, to have for such a statement? The temptation is to say that it can be reckoned to be true just in case either it has been or will eventually be conclusively established; and perhaps to add 'or else it has been or will come to be justified and not subsequently refuted'. Such an explanation would itself be circular, however: we should be explaining quantification over indefinite future time by quantification over indefinite future time. This difficulty forces us to recognize a feature of the notion of truth that is available under a justificationist theory of meaning, a feature of the utmost importance. The truth of some decidable statements ought not to be equated with their having been established, but should be regarded as obtaining independently of our knowledge, in virtue of our being in possession of an effective means of coming to know it. We cannot *in general* regard truth as a timeless property, however, that is, as one that, if

---

[1] A classic objection is that if the infinite task consists of denumerably many subtasks, and the times taken to perform the subtasks form a convergent series, such as 1 minute for the first, $\frac{1}{2}$ minute for the second, $\frac{1}{4}$ minute for the third, and so on, then those infinitely many subtasks will be completed in a finite time (in the example, in 2 minutes). In virtue of this, Russell said that running through the whole expansion of π in a finite time was medically, not logically, impossible (in 'The Limits of Empiricism', *Proceedings of the Aristotelian Society*, 36, 1935–6, at p. 143). It is not: it is a physical impossibility, and, as I think, a conceptual one. If the subtasks involve physical movement, and the distances traversed by them also form a convergent series, the task they together comprise can hardly be called infinite; but unless they form a convergent series, there will be a discontinuity of position at the moment at which the infinite task is completed.

possessed at all, has been possessed during all past time. The only conception of truth that we can have for a statement involving quantification over an infinite totality is that of its *having been* established. If it is a statement about indefinite future time for which we have no present grounds or evidence, then we must say that it *comes to be* true (if it does) but not that it may be, unknown to us, true already.

6

Tense and Time

A second operation that will carry a decidable sentence into an undecidable one is the conversion of the present tense into the past tense. The meaning of sentences in the past tense needs very careful consideration. If we directly apply to them justificationist considerations in their full rigour, we shall find ourselves forced to conclude that a past-tense statement can be true only if there are now memories or other traces of things' having been as it states. What makes this difficult to maintain are the links that bind the truth-value of an assertoric utterance made at one time with that of another, differently worded, made at another time. In particular, since it is true now that I am wearing a red tie, it must be true in exactly a year's time to say that just a year before I was wearing a red tie. On the face of it, this demonstrates that the truth of a statement in the past tense cannot depend upon the existence of present memories and traces of the past; for it may be that, in a year's time, everyone, including myself, will have forgotten what tie I was wearing on this day, and that all traces of my wearing one of that colour will have been obliterated.

It is not impossible to preserve these truth-value links while adopting a view of the past as having its whole substance in the present; but it compels us to adopt a very disagreeable metaphysical stance, according to which reality continually changes. Well, it may be said, reality *does* continually change, from moment to moment. But, according to the stance I have in mind, it would not be merely *the present* that continually changes: the present would drag the past, and push the future, with it. On this view, whatever we say can relate only to how things are *now*—and to how we *now* should judge them to have been in the past if we knew all the presently available evidence. If I now suppose that in a year's time someone will assert that I was wearing a red tie exactly a year before, I ought now, on this view, to endorse his statement as true, because I am *now* aware of wearing a red tie; I ought to do so, however few records of my present dress I suppose to survive until next year. But if, in a year's time, all traces of it have vanished, it will *then* no longer be correct to assert that I was wearing a red tie at this time. Or, rather, I cannot now say this: for I can now say only what is rendered true or false by how things now are. I should now say, rather, that such a assertion *will* be correct: but, surreptitiously, as it were, I shall know that, viewed from the perspective we shall have in a year's time, it will have lost the status of a correct assertion that it now possesses.

This is an intolerable position to adopt. It cannot, strictly speaking, be convicted of incoherence; but no one could possibly regard it as a credible conception of the world. The transition from the present tense to the past, or indeed the future, tense is not comparable to the replacement of a finite range of quantification by an infinite one. We may approach the problem by asking the question, irrelevant at first sight, what it is to understand a proper name such as 'Edinburgh' or 'Prince Charles'. A natural first answer is that it is to have a means for identifying the bearer of the name, or, in a truth-conditional theory, to know something that must hold good of an object for it to be the bearer. To determine whether a statement formed by inserting the name into the argument-place of some predicate is true or false, the bearer must be identified and then scrutinized to decide whether or not the predicate holds good of it, him, or her. But now, how is it with the name 'Napoleon'? Is it to know by what means an immensely aged man could be identified as Napoleon if we discovered that, amazingly, the Emperor had not died when we supposed, but had lived until the present? Could the canonical way of establishing the truth of a statement about Napoleon be followed only if this fantasy were true? Surely not. To understand the name 'Napoleon', one must know what the correct way, or at least *a* correct way, *was* to identify someone as Napoleon when he was alive.

In Prior's tense-logical semantics, a proposition is expressed by a type sentence. The basic type sentences, from which all others are formed, are in the present tense, or, more strictly, have tenseless main verbs; temporal indicators, whether mere past or future inflections of tense or an adverbial word or phrase such as 'two hours before', are treated as *sentential operators*. Whether this notion of a proposition is correct, or whether we ought to regard a proposition expressed by a sentence with an indexical indication of time as in part determined by the real or hypothetical time of utterance, is a question that we have seen we are free to settle at our convenience, and the second option is by far the more convenient.

Prior's treatment of tense is undoubtedly correct, however, as a representation of the way in which we acquire an understanding of it. We do not learn what it is for something to be brittle, say, at any arbitrary time, or to be wet at any arbitrary time, and then, learning what time is denoted by the adverb 'now', combine our two pieces of knowledge to yield a grasp of what it is for something to be brittle or to be wet now. Rather, we first learn what it is for something to be brittle or to be wet by learning to judge whether it is brittle or wet at the present time, and then apply to this our understanding of tense to make sense of saying that something will be brittle or was wet. A child very gradually learns how to build a temporal framework: first to speak of very recent or very imminent states of affairs, then of those some days previously or later that he has witnessed or will experience, then of events some years removed in time that adults remember or anticipate. A boundary is crossed unnoticed when he can make sense of talk about what happened or how things were before he was born; and then of talk about how things were before anyone whom he knows was born, and even before the human race existed. In a world in which all physical processes were immensely slower, so that what in fact takes a second took a year (or in which our psychological processes were immensely speeded, so that a second were experienced as having the duration that a year now has for us), the formation of this framework would probably be impossible; we could acquire no conception of past or future time. As it is, it is not difficult to see how a child forms that framework.

Further steps occur only in adulthood, and often not then. We say that a clock tells the time, and think of time as flowing equably, its flow measured by the clock. The picture is misleading: whatever we choose to treat as a clock *defines* whatever we are going to treat as durations of equal length. How, then, are we to make sense of a temporal location given in years, say, when the process that defines a year had not yet begun at that time, the solar system not then being in existence? Clearly, because the Earth's revolution about the Sun is not being treated for this purpose as the relevant clock. How can we attach a sense to speaking of the first four minutes, or the first four seconds, in the history of the Universe? Popular expositions of cosmology seldom trouble themselves to answer this question; an answer is obviously needed. The essential point, however, is that our grasp of the past tense consists in our ability to locate events within a *framework*, however that framework is established.

It is a mistake for a justificationist theorist of meaning to apply justificationist arguments to the interpretation of the past tense, treating the sense of a past-tense statement as given by what would justify its assertion at the time of making it. There is little temptation to do this for statements in the future tense, because it is natural to say that they are to be justified by waiting until the time to which they refer and then determining how things are at that time.

If, however, we succumb to the temptation for statements in the past tense, we shall view their senses as given by present memories and present traces of past events; but the truth-value link will then force us into a view of the past as itself changing, a view that we will have to acknowledge that we cannot meaningfully articulate. Rather, we have to see our understanding of tensed statements as derived from a twofold operation of our minds. We grasp what it is for the tenseless bases of those tensed statements to be true at any given time by having learned how they are to be recognized as holding good when applied to the present time; but, to understand the statements when the tense attached to them is not the present, we locate them within our temporal framework, apprehending them as saying how things were or will be at a temporal location other than that at which we now stand.

That this is an inescapably correct account of the matter follows from considering deductive reasoning about the past. A justificationist theory of meaning recognizes only constructive reasoning as valid. A constructive argument will lead from premises that can now be verified to a conclusion that can now be verified; it will furnish a means, given a present verification of the premises, to arrive at a present verification of the conclusion. When premises and conclusion are in the present tense, therefore, the property preserved from the former to the latter will be the possibility of establishing their truth. We cannot reasonably suppose, however, that a form of argument that would be valid if applied to statements about the present would lose its validity when applied to statements about the past; that the past is in some manner *more* indeterminate than the present. But empirical statements, unlike mathematical ones, are capable of losing the character of being verifiable or that of being decidable. If a conclusion, in the past tense, is derived by means of a constructive argument from premisses, also in the past tense, that were verified at the time to which they relate, it does not follow that it is now possible to verify the conclusion, still less that the conclusion was in fact verified at that time: only that the conclusion *could have been* verified at the time in question. A cylinder cuts a plane in an ellipse; hence, if *this* object has been measured and shown to be a cylinder, and *that* surface has been shown to be part of a plane, their intersection will be an ellipse, and this fact can be verified. So, if something was shown to be a cylinder and intersected a surface shown to be planar, their intersection must have been an ellipse; but, both cylinder and surface being gone, we can no longer verify this conclusion. If we were, as justificationists, to declare arguments about the past invalid unless they were guaranteed to lead to conclusions that could *now* be conclusively established, we should be allowing none but the most trivial of inferences to be drawn from facts about the past; in rejecting inferences parallel to ones we allow to be drawn from facts about the present, we should be denying that deductive reasoning could ever advance our knowledge of the past, in the sense in which it *can* advance our knowledge of the present or the future, or our knowledge of timeless mathematical facts. What goes for deductive reasoning must go, too, for past-tense forms of those decidable present-tense statements for which we admit bivalence. Bivalence must also hold for the past-tense counterparts of such statements, because, although they can no longer be decided, they could have been decided at the time. The number of people who witnessed the execution of Charles I must have been odd or even, although we cannot now tell which.

This may appear a large concession to realism. 'Why not go all the way, then?', many will be inclined to ask. This is the question of those who regard realism as the true faith, and are anxious to coax unbelievers into returning to it. But we should adhere to realism only to the extent that an accurate account of that understanding of the sentences of our language that underlies our use of them demands it. A blanket account of understanding a statement as knowing what it is for it to be true is useless, because circular: it attempts to explain what it is to grasp a thought in terms of having a thought about that thought. If there is any vindication of realism, it is not this. It is common ground that the earliest forms of sentence that we learn are decidable ones, such as 'It is foggy outside'; grasping what it is for statements made by their means to be true—for example, what it is for it to be foggy—can be agreed to consist in a capacity, when suitably placed, to decide them. As our language becomes more sophisticated, we learn to understand more complex forms of sentence. A scrutiny of what is needed to master the use of quantification over infinite totalities discloses no place for a notion of truth as applying to statements involving it independent of our grounds for ascribing truth to them, nor for a knowledge of what it is for them to be true independently of such grounds; so a straightforwardly justificationist account of them is called for. But the truth-value link does compel us to admit a place for a notion of truth for tensed statements independent of present evidence for them; we cannot construct a credible account of their use by interpreting the link as doing no more than barring us from ever assigning different truth-values to linked utterances made at different times. The philosopher's task is not to make a prior commitment for or against realism, but to discover where and how far realist considerations must be invoked in order to describe our understanding of our language: for they *may* be invoked only in so far as they *must* be invoked.

It may seem that we should speak, not of a temporal but of a spatio-temporal framework. Relativity considerations require us to classify, along with statements about the past, all those about events that we cannot in principle influence, nor they at present us: events outside our light-cone. An event predicted to happen in two years' time to the star Proxima Centauri falls into this category, since that star is four and a half light-years distant from the Sun. But our temporal and spatial concepts are bound together more tightly than by regarding time as one dimension among four. Our concept of distances greater than the reach of our limbs is closely connected with the time it takes to traverse them; this connection persists from primitive notions, like that of an hour's journey on foot, to sophisticated ones, like that of a light-year. An accurate account of the spatial frameworks we employ would not just echo what is to be said about our temporal one.

How, then, does a justificationist semantics, so far as we have yet reviewed it, bear upon the metaphysical view of reality that corresponds with it? We identified the truth of a proposition, not with our possessing a means of justifying an assertion of it, but with our having, or having had, a *capacity* to acquire such a justification. The resultant notion of truth constrains us to regard the world as determinate in respect of features that we have an effective means of determining, provided it is known that their outcome does not depend on any indeterminate factor.

If our language allowed us to frame only statements which, when suitably situated in time and space, we should have an effective means of deciding, there would be no difference between the logic consequent upon a realist or truth-conditional semantics for the language and a justificationist one: in both cases classical logic would be admitted as valid. The grounds for accepting that logic would indeed differ: the truth-conditional and the justificationist semantics would not coincide. Both would validate every instance of the law of excluded middle; but the justificationist semantics would reject bivalence for those propositions whose truth-value was never decided and that did not rest upon propositions known to have determinate truth-values. This would indeed create a difference in the metaphysics consequent upon these two semantic theories; but not a large difference, because the propositions about which they disagreed would be rather few in number.

A substantial divergence between the two theories arises because we can frame *un*decidable statements. The realist does not recognize any difference in principle between decidable statements and undecidable ones; but, in failing to perceive such a difference, he overlooks the basis for the concession to realism made by the version of justificationism here argued for. For many undecidable propositions, however, no compelling reasons for any such concession hold good. Nothing constrains us to attribute a determinate truth-value to a proposition to the effect that an event of a certain kind will at some time occur—say that a comet will collide with the Earth—so long as it remains possible but is neither realized nor inevitable. No more fundamental proposition is required also to be indeterminate in truth-value if indeterminacy is ascribed to the proposition involving quantification over all future time. A determinist, who holds that the entire future of the universe is contained in embryo in its present state, will indeed maintain that there must be such more fundamental propositions, even if he is unable to cite any; but, if we prescind from such metaphysical convictions, we have no reason to believe in their existence. I shall briefly discuss determinism in the next chapter; for the present, let us set it aside.

How do matters stand with counterfactual propositions? They, and subjunctive conditionals generally, are paradigmatic instances of undecidable propositions. Indeed, they are propositions to which we have little inclination to regard the principle of bivalence as applying. We are often impelled to wonder what would have happened if, at some turning-point of our lives, we had made a different decision; but reflection shows that there need be no definite answer to the question. Many other circumstances could have affected the outcome; there is no one thing that would have happened.

Does this apply to propositions concerning the outcome of some hypothetical measurement or test? If the measurement or test is carried out, it determines the magnitude of some quantity or the character of some object; many quantities are defined by how they are to be measured, and many properties by the test for their possession. In a vast range of cases, we take it for granted that, even if it was not measured, the given quantity had a determinate magnitude, and that, even if the test for possession of the property was not carried out, the object in question either possessed it or did not do so. The sense of an assignment to the quantity of a specific magnitude is then that of a counterfactual conditional, to the effect that, if a measurement had been carried out by any means, whether now available to us or not, it would have approximated that result; and similarly for an ascription to the object of the given property. Should we then deny that a proposition about what the result of a measurement or test would have been if it had been carried out, and any proposition that may be equated with such a counterfactual, is determinately true or false?

We have already looked at such a proposition: that concerning the number of apples in a certain basket. The result of a measurement or test is always decidable. Determining cardinal number by counting is analogous to determining the magnitude of a quantity by measurement; and we decided that we could *not* treat a proposition about the number of apples as lacking a determinate truth-value, even though the apples were not counted and could no longer be.

Yet counterfactual propositions do not in general satisfy bivalence. The question how So-and-so would have reacted if he had encountered me on a particular occasion need not have a determinate answer. Being rude and irascible, he might have insulted me, and might have lost his temper; but there may be no fact of the matter how he would actually have behaved. People do not have internal constitutions that determine how they will act in any given situation. Likewise, not every test could reasonably be thought to reveal an objective property. Tennis players undoubtedly differ in ability; but it would be superstitious to suppose that each possessed a determinate degree of skill, so that the outcome of every match was determined in advance. A match could not therefore be viewed as a test to show which of the two players was more skilled, for such a test would lack the predictive power required for the determination of an objective measure. For this reason, a counterfactual to the effect that, if two given players, of the same general level, were to play against one another, a particular one of them would win, could not be regarded as having a determinate truth-value.

Tests for physical properties, and measurements of physical quantities, such as the use of litmus paper as a test of acidity or alkalinity, are rightly regarded differently. The difference turns in part on the stability of the test: repeated trials by litmus paper of the same solution give the same result, whereas repeated matches between the same tennis players vary in their outcomes. If the matches always had the same outcome, we should conclude that one of the players was definitely better than the other, and treat this as an objective fact. But with physical properties and quantities there is another reason: science has to a large extent revealed their underlying basis. A property whose significance is purely human may be constituted by the past of an object. Someone may value a ring because it was the very one his father wore in his lifetime; if he lost it, he would not be consoled by being given an exact replica. There does not have to be any discernible difference from the ring he lost: the difference simply *is* that that was the ring his father wore. Wittgenstein toyed with the fantasy that indistinguishable seeds might grow into different plants solely because of their diverse origins; but we know that different behaviour on the part of inanimate objects can be due only to a difference in their *present* composition, not merely to a difference in their history. We can explain (or at least speculate about) the present physical link between past history and future behaviour. Once the link is established, our conception of the physical property changes: no longer is it a propensity to give a certain response to a test, but the underlying constitution that explains that response.

It is this fact that prompts us to treat physical tests with stable outcomes as revealing the possession of an objective property; and there can be no quarrel with our so regarding them. The objective status of the property tempts us to assume that a given object determinately either possesses or lacks it in all cases, including those in which the test is not performed; but, from a justificationist standpoint, that is not enough to guarantee such determinacy. Just as there are basic quantities, such as mass, so there are basic properties, such as shape; something may have *caused* an object to have the shape it has, but its having that shape is not *constituted* by its having any more basic properties. Given a justificationist theory of meaning, we can have no general reason for holding that any object must determinately either have possessed or have lacked a given basic property if the opportunity to observe or to test it for possession of that property was not taken and has now passed. But the line separating propositions not assured of a determinate truth-value and those that are assured of one does not run between those ascribing basic properties and those ascribing dependent ones—that is, properties the possession of which is constituted by the possession of more fundamental ones. All dependent properties are consequent, ultimately, on basic properties: if it is determinate whether an object has a dependent property, then it must be determinate whether it has a basic property on which the dependent property is consequent.

7

Reality As It Is In Itself

Our drive towards a realist interpretation of our language and hence of the world is very strong; naturally so, because our early experience compelled us to frame a conception of the objective features of reality, as revealed by our subjective apprehension of it. It goes against the grain to suppose that there may be no fact of the matter whether an object does or does not have a given property, or what the magnitude of a physical quantity may be. But that is the inescapable consequence of adopting a justification-ist theory of meaning. We have to relinquish the illusion that we know what it is for any proposition that we can frame to be true independently of our having any means of recognizing its truth, and settle for a conception of truth as depending upon our capacity to apprehend it.

It is never *totally* indeterminate what magnitude a given quant-ity has. Its magnitude must lie within some interval, which we can estimate with certainty, even if we carry out no measurement. What need not be determinate is the exact value of the mag-nitude within the given interval: indeed, if a precise magnitude is specifiable by an appropriate unit and a real number, it is *never* determinate what the magnitude of any quantity is. It is truistic that we can never measure any magnitude save to within an interval with rational end points; but this is usually conceived as a limitation upon human powers. We conceive of physical reality on the model of the classical continuum; all quantities, including temporal duration, have precise magnitudes, given, relatively to chosen units, by real numbers; it is just that our powers do not extend to their complete determination.

This model is certainly not derived from our experience of the world: it is a mathematical model that we *impose* upon reality; and the fit is very imperfect. A function from the real numbers to the real numbers is given by its value for each real number as argument. Unless the function is circumscribed in some way, its value for any argument is determined independently of its values for any other arguments. When the model is applied to physical reality, every feature of the physical universe is thought of as derivable from the magnitude, at each moment, of every basic quantity—that is, of every quantity not definable in terms of other quantities by arithmetical operations or by differentiation or integration. The imperfection of the fit is principally shown by the failure of this conception to display continuity in changes in the magnitudes of basic quantities as a conceptual, rather than a merely physical, necessity: the model allows descriptions that could have no physical realization. What should be taken as fundamental is not the magnitude of a basic quantity at a moment, but its, perhaps variable, magnitude over an interval, where this interval is not regarded as having precise end points. What is true of our determination of a magnitude—or of a point in time—is not due to a limitation on human powers; it is a feature of physical reality itself. A magnitude is something that lies within an imprecise interval, and may be capable of being determined to within a smaller interval, but does not possess a precise value given by a determinate real number.

It is for this reason that determinism is a fallacious doctrine. In a chaotic dynamical system, small variations in the boundary conditions, the initial parameters, will result in very large differences in the subsequent state of the system; for this reason, we cannot predict what that subsequent state will be. But it is normally supposed that such a system may be deterministic: given the exact values of the initial parameters, the subsequent state of the system is determined by the laws to which it is subject; our inability to predict it results only from the inescapable imprecision of our measurements. This reconciliation between unpredictability and determination rests upon the realist conception of reality after the model of the classical continuum: it assumes that the initial parameters must have precise values, given by real numbers. This assumption is a fantasy—a realist fantasy—which, though deeply embedded in our thinking, must be rejected. The supposition that a quantity has an *exact* magnitude, given, in terms of any selected unit, by a real number, which may be rational, algebraic, or transcendental, is a prototype of a proposition to which we have already said that no sense can be given: one that we could not in principle ever come to know. Once this fantasy has been rejected, the other fantasy, determinism, expires for lack of sustenance.[1]

We have thus learned two features of the notion of truth associated with a justificationist semantics. First, bivalence cannot be assumed to hold for all statements whose sense we can grasp. Specifically, it does not hold generally for undecidable statements whose truth is not constituted by the truth of decidable ones. We need a brief term for statements of this class: let us call them 'inaccessible' statements. We cannot claim, for every inaccessible statement that we do not know to be true and do not know to be false, that it nevertheless *is* determinately either one or the other. It follows that there may be fewer facts than a realist who subscribes to the principle of bivalence supposes. Reality is, or, rather, may be, in some respects indeterminate: there are intelligible questions that we can ask but to which there may be no answer—no fact of

---

[1] There can be a deterministic game in which the positions of the pieces are given not by real numbers but by rank and file on a chessboard. The initial layout of the pieces can be chosen at will, perhaps subject to a few constraints. In any lawful position, there will be one and only one legitimate move. But such a game would not be a model of the physical universe we inhabit.

the matter either way. A question asking for the exact magnitude of some quantity (where 'exact' is meant literally) must not be counted among these: since we *could* not know the answer, the question is not intelligible.

It is somewhat puzzling that many who believe the world to have been created adhere to the principle of bivalence. An author of fiction is not constrained to render determinate every detail of his fictional world; why should God be constrained in a way in which a human author is not? It may be answered that it is because God's creation is real, whereas the human author's world is only make-believe: but why should this difference affect the determinacy of their respective creations? It may be thought that, if there were no God and the world were uncreated, the contrast between real and fictional would supply a ground for complete determinacy: but, if the world has a Creator, then surely God is as much at liberty to leave some details of it undetermined as is a human author. The argument for the difference may be that, while you can describe something without specifying its size or its colour, you cannot make anything—say a toy kangaroo—without making it of a specific size and colour. Likewise, while what exists only fictionally may be indeterminate, as existing only in the incomplete description of it, what is real must be wholly determinate, whether or not there is a Creator. The argument, as applied to the universe conceived as uncreated, simply assumes what it aimed at proving. As applied to the universe conceived as created, on the other hand, it limits God's omnipotence unwarrantably. We can never establish any proposition as being neither true nor false, because for us something's not being true amounts to its being false—that is, to there being an obstacle to its truth. Hence we—at least those of us with unimpaired eyesight—cannot see anything save as being of some colour and some approximate size; and therefore we cannot make anything—anything that we can observe—save as of some colour and some approximate size. But, if God is the Creator of all that is in the universe, we ought not to think of Him as making things that, once made, exist self-subsistently and independently of Him. They exist only as conceived by their Creator, just as do the inventions of human creators of fiction. *We* can make a physical object only by manipulating some pre-existing matter; but God creates by His thought—'God said, "Let there be light", and there was light.' So, if God does not conceive of any part of His creation as fully determinate in all respects, it is not fully determinate.

Many people, being realists, conceive of reality as wholly determinate in all but one regard, but make a large exception of the future. They do not think that bivalence holds for statements in the future tense, or regard facts about the future as obtaining while it still is the future. The future is, for them, to a large degree, or even wholly, indeterminate; future-tense statements only *become* true or false at the time to which they relate, and hence, on their view, reality is cumulative as new facts come ever into existence. This way of thinking about the future is, however, flagrantly inconsistent with the realist standpoint. The realist believes that our grasp of the sense of any statement consists in a knowledge of what it is for it to be true. For a justificationist, a grasp of the sense of a statement consists in knowing how it can be recognized as true. If it is in the future tense, it can be conclusively recognized as true only at the time to which it relates, not that at which it is made; but that raises no problem about what our grasping its sense consists in. But, on a truth-conditional account of understanding, if a statement is incapable of being true, there is no such thing as knowing what it is for it to be true, and hence no such thing as grasping its sense: it can have no sense. A realist cannot, therefore, consistently espouse the view of future-tense statements as becoming true or false only at the time to which they relate; he must adopt the alternative conception according to which future facts obtain *already*, and are waiting for us to observe them when we arrive at the time in question.

But is not the justificationist in a similar position? I argued that he ought to view a grasp of the sense of a statement in the past tense as consisting in knowing, not how it can be established now or in the future, but how it could have been established at the time to which it relates. He does this because his understanding of tense is mediated by the temporal framework he has learned to construct. Does not this temporal framework extend towards the future? Ought he not, therefore, to conceive of statements about the future as *now* true or false according to whether they will be verified at the times to which they relate?

As an argument, this simply begs the question. If you doubt whether there is now any fact about whether some event will take place at a given time, you cannot be persuaded that there is a fact about whether it will be observed to take place at that time. It may be said that the same applies to the past. To a sceptic who thinks that there are no facts about what took place in the past other than those for which we have present evidence, it is useless to object that there are facts about what was or could have been observed to take place. I did not aspire to refute the sceptic's view: I merely pointed to its utterly unpalatable metaphysical consequences. The corresponding view about the future has no such consequences.

But what about the truth-value link? If it is true now to say 'A thunderstorm is now raging here', does not the truth-value link compel us to allow that, when Clara said yesterday 'There will be a thunderstorm here tomorrow', she would have said something true? It does indeed: but it does not compel us to say that what Clara said was *already* true at the time she said it. We now rightly judge what she said to have been true. We do so on the basis of what we now see and hear; but her statement *acquired* its truth at the time of the realization of her prediction.

I have argued that the notion of truth appropriate to a justificationist theory of meaning is asymmetrical as between past and future. Some feel a distaste for such asymmetry. But the aspect alters when we recognize that the contrast really lies between statements about events we cannot influence and those we could in principle influence or at least send information to: those outside and those within our future light-cone. So stated, there is no longer any asymmetry, strictly so called.

I am not arguing that no statements about the future can be true until the time to which they relate. Some events can be predicted with certainty, and any such prediction is true when made, as resting upon unquestionable evidence. The Christian faith includes the belief that the dead will be raised, and judged, and that thereafter there will be no additions to the human race. A Christian will judge a profession of this item of his faith to be true, as resting on divine revelation. It is only of uncertain statements about the future that we can say that they do not come to be true, if they do, until the time when they are fulfilled.

This, then, is the second feature of the metaphysics that follows from a justificationist conception of meaning: reality is cumulative. This is not only in virtue of the realization or falsification of predictions about the future. On a justificationist view, there is no legitimate notion of truth for inaccessible propositions other than their having been established as true. It is not merely that few statements about what will hold good at some future time can be established before that time; it is also that other statements may be established long after the time to which they relate, which had not previously been established. The facts that accumulate include ones about what held good before they came to be facts.

This is, of course, a paradoxical way of speaking. When we discover something about the past, we have only one temporal indicator to use in reporting it, and therefore speak of it as having held good from the time so indicated. For all that, we have, from a justificationist standpoint, no right to confuse the time *of* which it held good with the time *at* which our discovery conferred the status of fact upon it. The realist manner in which we naturally think of facts, or have been taught to think of them, is as immutable and independent of us. We *find out* some aspects of what is and always has been the case regardless of whether we were going to find it out or not. We are like blind men walking through a room, feeling the objects they encounter; objects that had long been there and would have been there even if the room had remained quite empty of people. This image is reinforced by the obvious recalcitrance of reality: we can choose to some degree what to attend to, but we cannot choose what we find when we attend to it. We do not create the world; we must accept whatever it presents to us.

Although facts indeed impose themselves upon us, however, we cannot infer from this that they were there waiting to be discovered before we discovered them, still less that they would have been there even if we had not discovered them. The correct image, on a justificationist view, is that of blind explorers encountering objects that spring into existence only as they feel around for them.

Our world is thus constituted by what we know of it or could have known of it. A realist might echo this saying, on the ground that, if a proposition is true, it might be known or have been known to be true. On a justificationist view, however, what we could have known extends only so far as the effective means we had to find out: the entailment is not from its being true to the possibility of knowing it, but in the opposite direction. It would be wrong to say that we *construct* the world, since we have no control over what we find it to be like; but the world is, so to speak, formed from our exploration of it.

The world of which I am speaking is *our* world, the world as we apprehend it. Our capacity to apprehend how the world is depends, of course, upon the concepts we possess—that is, upon our ability to describe it. We may speculate about beings who possess concepts that we lack. In virtue of the fact that we now have concepts that no one had five hundred years ago, this is not a fantasy: it becomes a fantasy when the concepts are conceived as ones we could never attain. New concepts, the result not of technological advance but of a deepening of our thought, are introduced to us by being *explained*—not, in general, defined—in the language we have at the time; the process is mysterious and deserves closer scrutiny.

But to suppose beings who manipulate concepts that we could *never* attain is problematic: how could we know that they really had any such concepts? If, all the same, the fantasy is allowed, what follows is that they inhabit a different world from ours: they apprehend the world in a way in which we cannot, and therefore it is not the same world, though doubtless one that intersects ours.

Does this not conflict with the distinction that is so fundamental to our outlook on the world, between how things appear to us and how they are in themselves? As a child grows up, he learns to apply this distinction in manifold ways. One of my daughters, when very small, once shook her head rapidly from side to side while looking at a street light, and said, 'Look what happens to the light when I do this': she thereupon learned a small lesson on the difference between how things appear and how they are. The urge to get behind the appearances and discover how things are in themselves remains with us: it is one of the motivations of science. And science has surely taught us a vast amount about how things are in themselves, including much that forms, for many who know little science and care little about it, the background to their conception of the world.

A clear example is our knowledge of what sound is. Creatures just as intelligent as ourselves, but who lacked the kind of curiosity we have, might have been content to accept sounds as just some among the many things that there happen to be in the world; but we wanted to know what sounds *are*. This knowledge now suffuses the least scientific person's conception of the world. In seeking to know this, we are no longer merely striving to attain the intersubjective, disentangled from the subjective; we are aiming to comprehend the external, disentangled from the internal. Our perceptual experience is determined jointly by the nature of our sense organs and by the impact on us of external reality. Sounds are what we hear; we want to know what the contribution of external reality is to our hearing them, what external events we apprehend in this manner. Only when our concept of a sound has been modified by our discovering this can it make sense to say, for example, that dogs can hear sounds too high in pitch to be perceptible by us.

What does it mean to speak of how things are in themselves? More exactly, what does it mean to speak of describing things as they are in themselves? Science progressively seeks descriptions in terms that do not depend, for their meaning, upon human modes of experience or upon the position of human beings in the universe. Our language is, of course, packed with terms that do depend upon these things; we could not learn it if it were not. The term 'up' is an obvious example. Primitively understood, up/down is one of the axes by reference to which the location of anything in the cosmos is determined; as soon as mankind grasped that the surface of the Earth is not approximately a plane, but closed, we recognized that 'up' and 'above', 'down' and 'below', denote directions only relatively to a position on the Earth's surface. A description in terms given meaning by the way we perceive reality is, to that degree, a description mediated by how things appear to us; we seek a description quite independent of our experience, knowing that that experience is determined in part by what we observe but in part also by our contingent sense organs, size, location, and other characteristics. We ask, 'What *is* sound?' and 'What *is* colour?', and then, 'What *is* light?'; sometimes we are baffled by the answers the physicists give us (how can anything be both a wave and a particle?). A more sophisticated kind of question is 'Is temporal precedence (or spatial distance) absolute or relative?' We are striving to find a description of the physical universe that is independent of our modes of observation.

To what goal does this progressive cleansing of our description of the world tend? It should arrive at an account of how things are in themselves, not depending at all upon the particular way we experience them or observe them directly or indirectly. When our descriptions have been completely purified, however, all that we are and can be left with are abstract mathematical models. Such purely abstract models are connected with our experience only at several removes; theory endows them with causal efficacy by using them to explain what we observe. As a scientific explanation, this is perfectly satisfactory: but what has happened to our ambition to know what things are like in themselves? It is not merely incredible that what there is in itself is a skeletal abstract structure: it does not so much as make sense to say that.

8

God and the World

The way things are in themselves is the only way in which they could be described if there were no sentient beings in the universe. What does that mean? Described by whom? Described by God, it might be answered. God has no particular point of view, no location *in* the world, no perspective contrasted with other perspectives. He knows, not by the effect of objects or events upon His perceptual equipment, but by His comprehension of all truth. How God apprehends things as being must be how they are in themselves.

The concept of the world as a whole is correlative to that of God, as standing over against the world. If that contrast is removed, no room remains for distinguishing the world as it is in itself from the world as we experience it and find it to be. There are indeed other sentient beings in the world: if not in near or remote galaxies, then at any rate here on Earth. They experience the world; but, since their sensory faculties differ, often greatly, from ours, and their intellectual capacities differ markedly also, they must inhabit different worlds from ours—worlds that intersect ours, but of which we can form only a hazy conception. We encounter them: we see them and they see us, we can touch or stroke them, they can bump into, bite, or sting us. But not only can we not describe their perceptual experience more than externally; we can gain only a confused idea of the concepts out of which their judgements about the world are built. It is not even clear whether the building blocks of those judgements are properly called 'concepts'. We cannot grasp what their worlds are like; if a lion could speak, we could not understand him.

But surely the 'worlds' of the various creatures are merely the partial and distorted projections of the one world, the world as it is in itself, upon the consciousness of those creatures. If the world is constituted by the totality of true propositions, this makes no sense. Propositions are built out of concepts; so a totality of propositions cannot be conceived independently of any particular intellectual resources comprising a conceptual vocabulary by means of which those propositions can be framed; and likewise the world as it is in itself cannot be conceived independently of how it is apprehended by any mind. What would it be for there to be a universe devoid of sentient beings? What would be the difference between God's creating a material universe, in the whole of which there never was any creature able to experience it, and His creating nothing at all? Or, rather, what would be the difference between His creating such a universe and His merely conceiving of it? What difference would its *existing* make? There would surely be no difference: for matter and radiation to exist is for it to be possible to perceive them or to infer their presence. There is nothing that would constitute the existence of a complex of radiation and of material objects if there were no beings to perceive any of it. That is not to say that there is no matter or radiation that is unperceived and uninferred; but, unless there are sentient and rational observers, it would not be *possible* for either observation or inference to occur.

But can we not imagine a universe devoid of sentient beings? We can imagine observing a world with no *other* observers in it; but that is not imagining a universe without observers. Is it then not possible to conceive of the world as we suppose it to be in itself, save for lacking sentient inhabitants? To conceive of it as it is in itself, under a description uncontaminated by any reference to human observational capacities, would be to conceive of an immensely detailed complex of mathematical structures, evolving in time in accordance with exceptionless or probabilistic laws. Certainly we can in principle conceive of such a complex, as we can conceive of other mathematical structures, including, if we wish, dynamic ones; but what would be added by specifying that *this* structure was not purely abstract, but actually *existed*? What substance would such a specification have? What is it for such a structure to exist in a more robust sense than that in which mathematicians assert the existence of a structure of this or that kind?

But was there not once just such a universe—a universe in which conditions rendered it impossible for there to be life anywhere within it? If the current beliefs of the cosmologists are sound, there was indeed: but this is nothing to the point. There is no logical law to the effect that, if something was once true, it is possible for it to have been true always and to go on being true always. Our world is constituted, not just by what we observe, but, more generally, by what we know of the world or could have known of it; and our knowledge derives not only from what we directly perceive, but also from what we infer from what we perceive. We have learned to make inferences from what we presently observe to how things were in the past, including those that invoke interpretations of what we observe in the light of far-reaching physical theories. We observe our universe to be such, if current cosmological theory is right, as to have had a beginning finitely long ago, followed by an era in which no part of it could have sustained life. The fact that neither in the remote past of the universe nor in its remote future did it or will it contain creatures capable of observing anything says nothing whatever about the intelligibility of conceiving of it as *never* being observed in its whole history.

The conception of 'the world as it is in itself' collapsed because, of our own resources, we can give no substance to the expression 'like' as it occurs in the question 'What is the world like in itself?' Our experience of the world is the resultant of the impact on beings contingently constituted in a particular way of the matter and radiation in the world surrounding them. By factoring out our particular constitution and spatio-temporal location, we seek to arrive at a pure presentation of the external factor. But to express our goal in this search by means of a word such as 'like' that calls for an account of experience, asking in effect how we should experience the world if we experienced it as it really is, and not in any particular way, is unintelligible: the question needs to be replaced by 'How is the world to be described as it is in itself?' This formulation shows very clearly the contradictory objective of our quest. We were seeking a description of reality that would be no mere description: a description of things as they *really* are, in themselves, and hence not framed within any particular vocabulary of concepts. Better expressed, we were seeking to attain a conception of the world not encapsulated in any description; for any description must employ a particular conceptual vocabulary, and any such vocabulary must reflect, and depend on, the particular way in which the world is apprehended by beings whose thoughts are framed within that vocabulary. But there can be no such thing; a conception of something can be mediated only by some manner of describing it. There is no way of conceiving anything independently of the store of concepts that determine the propositions we can entertain and of whose truth we judge.

That is why our search for a conception of the world as it is in itself ended with barren mathematical models of which it is senseless to think 'That is what there really is', still less 'That is *all* there really is'. We set out with a robust version of what is known as 'scientific realism' as our understanding of what science aims at: its task is, on this view, to uncover how things really are in themselves. We finished by relapsing into a purely instrumentalist interpretation: the mathematical models that physical theories postulate are to be accepted as providing a means of predicting what will be observed—of explaining it, too, as long as we are content to say that the models display how things are *at some level*—that is, at a level that is deepest only as judged by the order of this kind of explanation.

The dilemma cannot be simply resolved by abandoning any ambition to discover *the* world, as it can be characterized independently of us, and contenting ourselves with describing *our* world. For our knowledge of our world has layers, too; some descriptions of it, though of course framed in concepts that we grasp, owe less to our uninstructed experience than do others. Does 'our world' contain sounds, or does it contain only sound waves? Colours or only light of different wave-lengths? We express propositions by means of words whose senses are given to greater or lesser extent by reference to our perceptual experience; these senses determine the criteria whereby the various propositions are to be judged true or not true. When these criteria are satisfied, we rightly judge them to be true; but we cannot harmonize our judgements. Descriptions employing concepts given in very different ways appear to compete: they describe the *same* occurrences, but the descriptions stand at different levels. We are tempted to treat some of these descriptions as saying how things *really* are; but the temptation must be resisted. Not only because it leads eventually to the same barren result as before—a purely structural description lacking all substance—but also because a residue from a higher level remains unabsorbed when we descend to what appears to be a more basic level. The difficulty of accounting, at the more basic level, for the residue, and thus of harmonizing the different levels of description, gives rise to philosophical problems, expressed by asking 'Are there qualia?' or 'What is consciousness?' A solution is often sought by declaring each level of description valid in its own terms. If it is meant that each true proposition *is* true, and cannot be dismissed as not *really* or *ultimately* true, this is quite correct. If a statement is recognized as true according to the criteria for so recognizing it supplied by the meaning we have conferred upon it, then it is true, and there is no room for slighting the accolade of truth we have accorded it. But, if it is meant that descriptions of different levels do not in any way compete, the claim illegitimately evades the problem. We cannot harmonize what we rightly acknowledge as equally true descriptions; and, in so far as we cannot, we do not truly know even how to characterize our world.

We have reached the following uncomfortable position. We cannot conceive of the world in complete independence of the manner in which we apprehend it, although we acknowledge that other creatures apprehend it differently. We have only the haziest notion of how such other creatures apprehend the world; yet we are debarred from forming a conception of 'the world' that we and they all apprehend in such different ways, precisely because such a conception would be independent of any particular way of apprehending it. We can make no clear sense of there *being* a world that is not apprehended by any mind. Worse, yet, we ourselves do not really have any single conception of the world. We have a number of different conceptions, and know which one to make use of for each of our various purposes, but are unable to harmonize them into a single unified conception.

We described animals and possible other sentient or rational denizens of the universe as inhabiting worlds distinct from ours but intersecting it. The common-sense view is that they inhabit the same world, but, having different sense organs and employing different concepts, they apprehend it differently. This 'same world' has to be the 'world as it is in itself' that we feel so strong a drive to discover how to describe; and the reason for the more romantic, and more obscure, way of putting the matter is precisely that the notion of the world as it is in itself, rather than as it is perceived or intellectually grasped, appeared to crumble and to prove incoherent. And yet there must be a way of validating that notion; without it there remains only a jumble of different worlds, our own and those of other creatures, which cannot be coherently related to one another.

Since it makes no sense to speak of a world, or the world, independently of how it is apprehended, this one world must be the world as it is apprehended by some mind, yet not *in any particular way*, or from any one perspective rather than any other, but simply as it is: it constitutes the world as it is in itself. We saw that how God apprehends things as being must be how they are in themselves. But now we must say the converse: how things are in themselves consists in the way that God apprehends them. That is the only way in which we can make sense of our conviction that there is such a thing as the world as it is in itself, which we apprehend in certain ways and other beings apprehend in other ways. To conceive of the world as it is in itself requires conceiving of a mind that apprehends it as it is in itself.

God and the world stand over against one another; more exactly, our concepts of God and of the world as a whole stand over against one another. There is no possibility of conceiving the world as a single reality, apprehended differently by different creatures within it, otherwise than as known in its totality by a mind that apprehends it as it is. We are the only terrestrial creatures to apprehend the world otherwise than as it presents itself to our senses, through our knowledge gained by observation, calculation, experiment, and theory, and yet we cannot frame a unified conception of reality, either scientifically or philosophically. There can be a unitary reality that all sentient creatures apprehend in their particular ways only if there is a mind that comprehends it completely as it is in itself; and we can give no sense to speaking of reality as it is in itself save as apprehended by such a mind.

This does not imply that God understands what it is for the material universe to exist independently of there being within it any sentient creatures to perceive it. His understanding of the material universe must conform to the principle that for matter and radiation to exist is for it to be possible to perceive them or to infer their presence. God, who knows everything as it is, does not need to make inferences; and perception, which requires sense organs, cannot be the mode of His knowledge. His knowledge of how matter is disposed is not an instance of *observation*, as of the tree in the quad in the limerick; it is a knowledge of what the sentient beings that the universe contains will observe. God's knowledge of the material universe consists in the grasp of an immensely complex structure determining what will be observed by the various kinds of sentient creatures, according to the kinds of sense organ they possess and their location in the cosmos, and what will be discovered by the various rational creatures when they attempt to find out what things are in themselves; their sense organs and their locations are themselves parts of the structure.

This structure, as God conceives it, *is* the world as it is in itself; no other sense can be allotted to that phrase. Since God's knowledge of how things are *constitutes* their being as they are, He is rightly called Creator; this applies as much to His knowledge of the propositions we can frame and to whose truth we can attain as to His knowledge of those framed and recognized as true by other inhabitants of the universe, but lying beyond our grasp. It is only in virtue of God's constituting the truth of all these propositions by His knowledge of them that we can regard all sentient creatures as dwellers in the *same* world.

Some liken God's knowledge with our knowledge in intention of what we are doing or what we shall do in the future. It might appear out of place to make such a comparison here, however; for nothing has so far been argued to justify the attribution to God of a *will*, nor, therefore, of intentions, motives, or purposes. It is natural to think that, if philosophy is able to support the conception of God as having a will, it must be in view of considerations different from those that have here been discussed; indeed, I said as much in the original lecture on which this chapter is based. The question 'What makes things to be as they are?' is answered by reference to God's knowledge. But, unless it is possible to attribute a will to God, the question '*Why* are things as they are?' cannot be answered by 'God wills, or at least permits, them to be so'.

Whoever has a will must be capable of action. God acts, since He is Creator: things are as they are because by thought alone

He makes them to be so. According to the view argued for in the preceding chapter, physical quantities possess a magnitude only within a certain interval (though this may be very small). The effects of two similar physical events may therefore differ, consistently with the physical laws that govern them: it must be the will of God that determines what they shall be, within the range of effects consistent with those laws. Even for those who adhere to the super-realist notion, to which indeed most people mistakenly cleave, of a precise though undiscoverable magnitude for every quantity, and do not understand quantum mechanics as involving any genuine indeterminacy, it remains that God is the Creator of the physical universe as a whole, and hence the giver of the laws that govern it. Creation is an act, and the imposition of laws is an act: God therefore possesses the first qualification for having a will.

When people speak of God as Creator, they often entertain absurd imagery. They connect creation with initiation, whereas it truly has no more to do with the first than with any later moment; a cloudy recognition of this is expressed by those who say that God created the universe and subsequently sustains it in being. The chief inapposite image is that of God as existing through endless time over against an empty universe, and at some moment during that time performing an act of creation whereby the universe is filled with creatures. This is nonsense. If the universe has a finite age, then time has an absolute zero. Time is the measure of change, and it makes no sense to speak of how things were before there was anything that changed; that is, in effect, to speak of how they were at some moment earlier than the earliest moment. 'Before' is a temporal word, save when it is used in a transferred sense as relating to some non-temporal ordering—for instance, as the inverse of 'dependent on'. Since it can be right to speak of times only as those at which events occurred, it must be correct to say that the universe has always existed, whether its age is finite or infinite. If it makes sense to speak of God as existing at one time or another, then of course God has always existed; but it is senseless to speak of Him as existing *before* there was any time.

In any case, it seems doubtful that an absolute sense can be attributed to the question whether the universe has a finite age. Ascribing any specific finite age to it depends upon calibrating time, so that the notion of a second's duration can be applied to conditions utterly different from those that now obtain. Given any such calibration, a new one can always be derived from it so that the age of the universe becomes infinite, although no new events have been postulated. Conversely, given a calibration that brings out the age of the universe as infinite, it can always be revised so as to render it finite. It seems dubious that there can be an absolute sense in which one calibration is the only correct one. If some physical process, neutron decay or whatever, is nominated as the clock, it of course becomes impossible to question whether that process always takes the same time. But clearly no authority determines which process shall be so nominated, or that any shall be. It is a matter of which choice proves to yield the smoothest mathematical description of physical interactions.

For a being to have a will, that being must not only be capable of action, but be capable of selecting an action to perform out of a range of possible alternatives. As we saw, God acts, and, in doing so, obviously makes a choice out of many possibilities. Moreover, for a being to have a will in a full sense, that being, in choosing between alternative possible actions, cannot in all cases be choosing arbitrarily. Sometimes it is necessary to make an arbitrary choice, as Buridan's ass failed to understand; but, since there is usually a significant difference between possible actions or between their consequences, the choice will usually be made for a reason. Since the consequences of different choices would often be very different, we must suppose that God's choices between different possible actions must be guided by His apprehension of those consequences: God must have motives for His actions. And thus we may ascribe to God a will in the fullest sense of the concept. When the disciples of Jesus were taught to say 'Thy will be done', they were not being induced to make a vacuous prayer.

Can God's will be thwarted? It might seem that this is impossible, since evidently God has the power to prevent it. Yet, if the Ten Commandments, or anything resembling them, represent God's will for us—His will for how we should conduct ourselves—that will is manifestly thwarted repeatedly and massively. We can resolve this only by distinguishing between God's immediate will and His overall will. It must be His will, all things considered, that we should be free to flout His immediate will—to commit murder and adultery, to lie and act cruelly—rather than that we should conform to that immediate will perforce.

But what about what appears contrary to God's will, but is not due to human wickedness? Terrible suffering caused by disease or natural disaster, for example, or the suffering of plainly sentient creatures seized by their predators. Is God unconcerned about the well-being of His sentient creatures? 'The lions roaring after their prey do seek their meat from God,' the Psalmist affirms; but the prey do not receive what they seek when the lions are successful in the hunt. The Old Testament has also a different tradition. In Genesis neither man nor the beasts are assigned flesh as their food, but only the fruits of the earth; and in the famous prophecy of Isaiah, in which the lion eats straw like the ox, the prophet says, 'They shall not hurt or destroy in all my holy mountain.' Clearly there was a perception that the violence that prevails within the animal kingdom (man included) is contrary to the immediate will of God. That it does prevail must be due to some overriding necessity. We cannot say that we shall never know what that necessity is. Some clever person might divine it; or it might be the subject of a revelation from God. But we cannot say for sure that we shall know what it is; as we are now, it is almost certainly beyond us to divine what the necessity may be. The atheist of course here gains a local argumentative advantage, for he need not suppose that there is anything we do not know and cannot guess: the forces of natural selection produce animals that prey on other animals, and that is that.

Realizing that the notion of the world as it is in itself can be given substance—namely, as the world as God knows it to be—does not help us to harmonize the truths, at different levels, which we know to hold good concerning our world; nor should it deter us from striving to achieve the best description we can attain of the world with the minimum of appeal to our experience in order to explain the meaning of that description. It will, however, ease our anxiety over our failure to harmonize all our knowledge or to attain a satisfying neutral description, by making us understand that such failure may be, in the nature of things, inevitable. What we must resist is the temptation to invoke God's knowledge as a guarantee of bivalence or of precise magnitudes for all quantities. Faced with a question we cannot answer, a justificationist semantics returns the discouraging reply that there may not *be* an answer, though we can never rule out the possibility that there is one. When there is an answer that we do not know, we may say that God knows it: He knows it because, for every true proposition, He knows that it is true. But we have no right to assume that, for every intelligible question, God knows an answer to it; if there *is* no answer, there is nothing for Him to know. God does not need to know what any given rational beings would observe or discover if they were to make such-and-such investigations that in fact they will never make; such counterfactual questions need have no determinate answer.

The cumulative character of truth presents a problem. If you, telling me an experience you had, say, 'I thought, "I don't know where I am"', neither of us can now *think* that thought, but we both know what thought you had. Likewise, although our thoughts are not God's thoughts, He knows what thoughts we have. Now, when we say that God exists, or that God knows one or another thing, is the tense we use a genuine present, or do the verbs 'to exist' and 'to know' have 'the tense of timelessness', as Frege called it? If we are using a genuine present tense, then God is in time; and this implies that some things may be true of Him at one time that were not true before. He may then change in respect of what He knows. This does not infringe His omniscience: God always knows everything that is true, but some propositions become true that were not true before. Such a degree of change in God is in grave tension with the changelessness that is part of our concept of God. Can we say that God does not change *in Himself*, but can change in what He knows about things other than Himself, in the way that we do not say that the number 3 has changed when the three children in a family acquire a sibling? Three was the number of children in the family, and is so no longer; but the change is extrinsic, not intrinsic. This might be satisfactory if God's knowledge, like our own, were dependent on the reality He knows; but it is the other way about—the reality depends upon His knowing it to be as it is.

We must therefore adopt the alternative, that, when we speak of God's knowledge, we are using the tense of timelessness. God can distinguish between those of our thoughts that we shall later recognize as true or as false, and those that will never be verified or falsified. It may appear that, on this assumption, a notion of truth, for propositions that we can grasp, becomes available to us that goes beyond what we can now recognize as true: a proposition is true in this sense if God knows that we shall recognize it as true. Such a notion of truth would support a principle of trivalence at odds with the intuitionistic logic that is ordinarily in accordance with a justificationist semantics: propositions would be divisible, by reference to God's knowledge, not our own, into those that are or will be true, those that are or will be false, and those for ever indeterminate; we should need, not an intuitionistic, but a three-valued, logic. This is an illusion, which arises from reading the verb 'knows', in the phrase 'God knows whether...', as being in the genuine present tense—that is, as meaning 'God *now* knows whether...'. If 'knows' is in the tense of timelessness, we cannot so read it; and so we cannot by this means extract a new notion of *present* truth. The only notion of truth available to us remains the justificationist notion.

God needs to make no inferences; but it could be argued that the divine logic must be three-valued. If there are no gaps in reality, that is, no questions that have no answers, then God's logic will be classical. Those many people who favour classical over intuition-istic logic are therefore guilty of the presumption of reasoning as if they were God.

Index